Steck-Vaughn

English ASAP™

Connecting English to the Workplace

O9-BTO-473

SCANS Consultant

Andrea Perrault
Connected Resources—Learning that Works!
Boston, Massachusetts

Program Consultants

Judith Dean-Griffin
ESL Teacher
Windham Independent School District
Texas Department of Criminal Justice
Huntsville, Texas

Marilyn K. Spence
Workforce Education Coordinator
Orange Technical Education Centers
Mid-Florida Tech
Orlando, Florida

Brigitte Marshall
English Language Training
for Employment Participation
Albany, California

Dennis Terdy
Director, Community Education
Township High School District 214
Arlington Heights, Illinois

Christine Kay Williams
ESL Specialist
Towson University
Baltimore, Maryland

STECK-VAUGHN®
C O M P A N Y

A Division of Harcourt Brace & Company

Acknowledgments

Executive Editor: Ellen Northcutt

Supervising Editor: Tim Collins

Assistant Art Director: Richard Balsam

Interior Design: Richard Balsam, Jill Klinger

Electronic Production: Jill Klinger, Stephanie Stewart, David Hanshaw, Alan Klemp

Assets Manager: Margie Foster

Editorial Development: Course Crafters, Inc., Newburyport, Massachusetts

Illustration Credits:

Cover: Tim Dove, D Childress

Cindy Aarvig–p.20b, 22-24, 25e, 109d-e; Richard Balsam–p. 90c, 97g-h; Barbara Beck–p.75, 77, 87; Antonio Castro (Represented by Cornell & McCarthy, LLC)–p.30, 32d-e, 34, 40a, 42a, 71, 76a, 78a, 82a, 92a, 94, 101, 109a-c; Chris Celusniak–p.51, 69b, 73d-f, 89, 91b-e, 108b-e; David Griffin–p.16, 18a, 21b-d, 25a-d, 52, 67, 72a, 99, 100, 107, 114, 116; Dennis Harms–p.32a-c, 60a, 96; Chuck Joseph–p.36, 39d-f, 46b-g, 47b-d, 49d-f; Linda Kelen–p.106; Michael Krone–p.6, 8, 10, 15a-d, 20a, 27, 37, 44a, 44c-d, 46a, 76b-d, 93, 102, 111; Annie Matsick (Represented by Cornell & McCarthy, LLC)–p.28, 29, 33b-g, 64, 68a, 73a-c, 80a, 87, 88, 95; Gordon Ricke–p.63; John Scott–p.11a-b, 56, 58a, 61, 66, 70a, 90a, 91a, 97a-f, 104a, 112, 113b-d; Charles Shaw–p.2, 14, 26, 38, 50, 62, 74, 86, 98, 110; kreativ-design/Danielle Szabo–p.2, 3, 4b-c, 5, 9a-b, 11c-e, 12-14, 15e-h, 18b-e, 21a, 26, 33a, 35, 37e, 38, 39a-c, 40b-c, 42b, 43, 44b, 45, 47a, 48, 49a-c, 50, 53, 55, 57, 58b-c, 59, 60b-c, 62, 68b-e, 70b-d, 72b, 74, 78b, 79, 80b-d, 81, 82b, 83, 84, 85d, 86, 90b, 92b-d, 98, 104b, 105, 108a, 110, 113a, 115, 117-121; Victoria Vebell–p.54.

Contents

About SCANS, the Workforce, and *English ASAP: Connecting English to the Workplace*

SCANS and the Workforce

The Secretary's Commission on Achieving Necessary Skills (SCANS) was established by the U.S. Department of Labor in 1990. Its mission was to study the demands of workplace environments and determine whether people entering the workforce are capable of meeting those demands. The commission identified skills for employment, suggested ways for assessing proficiency, and devised strategies to implement the identified skills. This commission's first report, entitled *What Work Requires of Schools—SCANS Report for America 2000*, was published in June 1991. The report is designed for use by educators (curriculum developers, job counselors, training directors, and teachers) to prepare the modern workforce for the workplace with viable, up-to-date skills.

The report identified two types of skills: Competencies and Foundations. There are five SCANS Competencies: (1) Resources, (2) Interpersonal, (3) Information, (4) Systems, and (5) Technology. There are three parts contained in SCANS Foundations: (1) Basic Skills (including reading, writing, arithmetic, mathematics, listening, and speaking); (2) Thinking Skills (including creative thinking, decision making, problem solving, seeing things in the mind's eye, knowing how to learn, and reasoning); and (3) Personal Qualities (including responsibility, self-esteem, sociability, self-management, and integrity/honesty).

Steck-Vaughn's *English ASAP: Connecting English to the Workplace*

English ASAP is a complete SCANS-based, four-skills program for teaching ESL and SCANS skills to adults and young adults. *English ASAP* follows a work skills-based syllabus that is compatible with work skills in the CASAS and MELT competencies. *English ASAP* has these components:

Student Books

The Student Books are designed to allow from 125 to 235 hours of instruction. Each Student Book contains 10 units of SCANS-based instruction. A Listening Transcript of material appearing on the Audiocassettes and a Vocabulary list, organized by unit, of core workforce-based words and phrases appear at the back of each Student Book. Because unit topics carry over from level to level, *English ASAP* is ideal for multilevel classes.

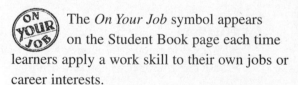 The *On Your Job* symbol appears on the Student Book page each time learners apply a work skill to their own jobs or career interests.

Teacher's Editions

The Teacher's Editions provide reduced Student Book pages with answers inserted and wraparound teacher notes that give detailed suggestions on how to present each page of the Student Book in class. Teacher's Editions 1 and 2 also provide Blackline Masters to reinforce the grammar in each unit. The Literacy Level Teacher's Edition contains Blackline Masters that provide practice with many basic literacy skills. The complete Listening Transcript,

Vocabulary list, charts for tracking individual and class success, and a Certificate of Completion appear at the back of each Teacher's Edition.

Workbooks

The Workbooks, starting at Level 1, provide reinforcement for each section of the Student Books.

Audiocassettes

The Audiocassettes contain all the dialogs and listening activities in the Student Books.

 This symbol appears on the Student Book page and corresponding Teacher's Edition page each time material for that page is recorded on the Audiocassettes. A Listening Transcript of all material recorded on the tapes but not appearing directly on the Student Book pages is at the back of each Student Book and Teacher's Edition.

Workforce Writing Dictionary

Steck-Vaughn's *Workforce Writing Dictionary* is a 96-page custom dictionary that allows learners to create a personalized, alphabetical list of the key words and phrases they need to know for their jobs. Each letter of the alphabet is allocated two to four pages for learners to record the language they need. In addition, each letter is illustrated with several workforce-related words.

Placement Tests

The Placement Tests, Form A and Form B, can be used as entry and exit tests and to assist in placing learners in the appropriate level of *English ASAP.*

Placement

In addition to the Placement Tests, the following table indicates placement based on the CASAS and new MELT student performance level standards.

Placement

New MELT SPL	CASAS Achievement Score	English ASAP
0–1	179 or under	Literacy
2–3	180–200	Level 1
4–5	201–220	Level 2

Using this Book in Multilevel Classes

English ASAP Literacy Level can be used in a variety of ways in multilevel classes. Here is a suggested procedure.

◆ Present to the class as a whole the oral and aural activities for the day in Level 1 of *English ASAP.*

◆ Meet with the literacy learners as a group for the reading and writing instruction in the Literacy Level Student Book as the Level 1 learners complete the exercises in their Student Books and Workbooks.

◆ When the literacy learners are ready to begin the independent or paired activities in their books, check the Level 1 learners' work or provide them with additional instruction.

About the Literacy Level

Organization of a Unit

Each of the ten units follows a consistent whole-part-whole organization.

◆ The Unit Opener's illustrations and accompanying questions introduce the unit topic and preview the SCANS skills covered in the unit.

◆ The Getting Started page uses interactive activities and peer teaching to introduce the new language in the unit.

- Four teaching spreads systematically present the new material in the unit.

- The Extension page allows for integration and expansion of the new language, literacy skills, and SCANS skills.

- The Performance Check page allows teachers to assess learners' progress and to determine whether any additional reinforcement is needed.

Unit Opener

Each Unit Opener includes four large, engaging illustrations and accompanying questions. Each illustration depicts people using the unit's target language, literacy skills, and SCANS skills. Situations include people applying for jobs, completing forms, interacting with coworkers and supervisors, using technology at work, and assisting customers. The illustrations and questions activate learners' prior knowledge by getting them to think and talk about the unit topic. To stimulate discussion, follow these suggestions:

- Encourage learners to say whatever they can about the illustrations. Prompt them by indicating objects for them to name. You might also identify and say the names of objects, places, and people for them to point to and repeat. Write key words on the board.

- Help learners read any signs or words that are visible.

- Have learners answer the questions. Repeat their answers or restate them in acceptable English.

Getting Started

An initial teamwork activity presents the key work skills, concepts, and language introduced in the unit. Critical thinking and peer teaching activities activate the use of the new language and preview the content of the unit. A partner work activity encourages learners to use the new language in communicative ways.

Teaching Spreads

Each of the four teaching spreads presents one or more literacy skill and SCANS skill. *English ASAP* Literacy Level takes a recognition-word approach to teach letters and words in meaningful, communicative contexts. Learners learn to read and write only the words that they need to master the unit SCANS skills.

- The recognition words for each spread are presented at the top of the first page of that spread. For information on presenting recognition words, see "Presenting Recognition Words" on page viii.

- The first activity on each spread is usually a short dialog that presents the spread's recognition words in context. As learners listen to and say each dialog, they gain valuable experience using the new language. For detailed instructions, see "Presenting Dialogs" on page viii.

- Exercises give learners experience in reading and writing the recognition words in isolation and in context.

- The complete alphabet is presented in the first six units. The letters are usually included in the spread's recognition words. Thus, learning the alphabet becomes a meaningful, relevant task. Exercises give learners experience in writing letters in isolation and in the context of familiar SCANS-based words. For suggestions on teaching the letters, see "Presenting Letters" on page viii.

- Listening and speaking activities appear throughout the teaching spreads, allowing learners to develop all four language skills. The paired speaking activities get learners talking from the start. Listening tasks include listening for addresses, telephone numbers, names of work supplies, locations, days of the week, dates, times, and prices.

All of the listening activities develop the skill of **focused listening.** Learners learn to recognize the information they need and to listen selectively for only that information. They do not have to understand every word;

rather, they have to filter out everything except the relevant information. This essential skill is used by native speakers of all languages when listening to their own languages.

◆ Culminating activities on each spread allow learners to use their new literacy skills, and include reading or filling in pieces of realia such as job applications or checks, practicing dialogs, and completing writing activities.

Extension

Following the teaching spreads, the Extension page enriches the previous instruction. As in other sections, realia is used extensively. Oral and written exercises help learners master additional skills, language, and concepts, and relate them to their workplaces and career interests.

Performance Check

Each unit concludes with a one-page Performance Check, which is designed to allow teachers to track learners' progress and to meet their school's or program's learner verification needs. Skills are tested in the same manner that they are presented in the units, so formats are familiar and nonthreatening, and success is built in. For more information on this section, see "Evaluation" on page ix.

Teaching Techniques

Make Your Classroom Mirror the Workplace

Help learners develop workplace skills by setting up your classroom to mirror a workplace. Use any of these suggestions.

◆ Establish policies on lateness and absence similar to those a business might have.

◆ Provide learners with a daily agenda of the activities they will complete that day including partner work and small group assignments. Go over the agenda with learners at the beginning and end of class.

◆ With learner input, establish a list of goals for the class. Goals can include speaking, reading, and writing English every day; using effective teamwork skills; or learning ten new vocabulary words every unit. Go over the goals with learners at regular intervals.

◆ Assign regular jobs and responsibilities to learners, such as arranging the chairs in a circle, setting up the overhead projector, or making copies for the class.

Presenting a Unit Opener

The unit opener sets the stage for the unit. Use the illustrations and questions to encourage learners to speculate about what the unit might cover, activate prior knowledge, and relate what they see in the illustrations to their own work environments.

Peer Teaching

Because each adult learner brings rich life experience to the classroom, *English ASAP* is designed to help you use each learner's expertise as a resource for peer teaching.

Here are some practical strategies for peer teaching:

◆ Have learners work in pairs/small groups to clarify new language concepts for each other.

◆ If a learner possesses a particular work skill, appoint that learner as "class consultant" in that area and have learners direct queries to that individual.

◆ Set up a reference area in a corner of your classroom. Include dictionaries, career books, and other books your learners will find useful.

Partner Work and Teamwork

The abundance of partner work and teamwork activities in *English ASAP* serves the dual purposes of developing learners' communicative competence and providing learners with experience using key SCANS interpersonal skills, such as working in teams, teaching others, leading, negotiating, and working well with people from culturally diverse backgrounds. To take full advantage of these activities, follow these suggestions.

- Whenever learners work in groups, appoint, or have learners select, a leader.

- Use multiple groupings. Have learners work with different partners and teams, just as workers do in the workplace. For different activities, you might group learners according to language ability, work skill, or learner interest.

- Make sure learners understand that everyone on the team is responsible for the team's work.

- At the end of each activity, have teams report the results to the class.

- Discuss with learners their teamwork skills and talk about ways teams can work together effectively. They can discuss how to clarify roles and responsibilities, resolve disagreements effectively, communicate openly, and make decisions together.

Presenting Dialogs

To present the dialogs, follow these suggested steps.

- Establish meaning by having learners talk about the illustration. Clarify all the new vocabulary in the dialog using pictures and pantomime.

- Play the tape or say the dialog aloud two or more times.

- Say the dialog aloud line-by-line for learners to repeat chorally and then individually.

- Have learners say the dialog together in pairs.

- Have several pairs say the dialog aloud for the class.

Presenting Recognition Words

To present each recognition word, first clarify the meaning of the word. Display the object or a picture card, or use the picture on the Student Book page. Say the word and have learners repeat. Then display a word card with the word on it. Say the word. As you say it, sweep your hand under the word. Have learners repeat. Display the word card and the picture card at random and have the class say or read the word chorally each time. Continue until the class can respond with ease. Then have individuals respond.

Reinforcing Vocabulary

To provide additional reinforcement of the recognition words, use any of these suggestions.

- **Steck-Vaughn's *Workforce Writing Dictionary*.** Learners can use Steck-Vaughn's *Workforce Writing Dictionary* to create a completely customized lexicon of key words and phrases they need to know.

- **Flash cards.** Flash cards are easy for you or your learners to make. Write a new word or phrase on the front of each card. Put a picture of the object or action on the back of the card. Learners can use the cards to review vocabulary or to play a variety of games, such as Concentration.

- **The Remember-It Game.** Use this simple memory game to review the vocabulary of any topic. For example, to reinforce names of places at work, start the game by saying, *We're going to the office*. The next learner has to repeat what you said and add a place. For example, he or she may say, *We're going to the office and the break room*. If someone cannot remember the whole list or cannot add a word, he or she has to drop out. The learner who can remember the longest list wins.

Presenting Letters

Use letter cards with both capital and lower-case letters on them to present the letters. Hold up each card, say the name of the letter, and have learners repeat. Point out the difference between capital and lower-case letters. Write the capital and lower-case letters on the board and trace them with your finger. Have learners trace the strokes in the air. Next, have learners open their books and trace the letters with their fingers and with their pencils. Then have them write the letters on the lines. Use Blackline Masters 2, 3, and 5 in the Teacher's Edition to provide additional reinforcement.

Environmental Print

As learners learn new letters, encourage them to find examples of the new letters in the room around them. You might ask them to find examples in old magazines, in items in their purses or wallets (such as driver's licenses or work permits), on signs in the room, or on objects visible from the window.

Presenting Listening Activities

Use any of these suggestions to present the listening activities.

◆ Help learners read the directions.

◆ Model the activity. Write the example item on the board and complete it as you play the tape or read the Listening Transcript of the first item aloud.

◆ Play the tape or read the Listening Transcript aloud as learners complete the activity. Rewind the tape and play it again as necessary.

◆ Check learners' work.

Evaluation

To use the Performance Check page successfully, follow these suggested procedures:

Before and during each evaluation, create a relaxed, affirming atmosphere. Chat with the learners for a few minutes and review the material with them. Make sure that everyone has a pen or a pencil. When you and the learners are ready, help learners read the directions and look over each exercise before they complete it. Then have learners complete the activity. If at any time during the process you sense that the learners are becoming frustrated, feel free to stop the evaluation process to provide additional review. You might have learners turn back to the page where the material was presented. Resume when learners are ready. Check learners' work. The Teacher's Edition contains reproducible charts for you to copy and use to keep track of individual and class progress.

To the Teacher

Steck-Vaughn

English ASAP™

Connecting English to the Workplace

Steck-Vaughn

Look at the pictures.

What do you see?

Where are they?

Getting Started

Write the letter.

Frost Foods

Application for Work

a

b

Name: __Nancy Lake__   Telephone Number: __555-5645__

Address: __11__   __Main Street__
          Number   Street

c

__Los Angeles__   __California__   __93221__
  City   State   Zip Code

d   e   f

___c___ **1.** Address   _____ **2.** Name   _____ **3.** State

_____ **4.** Zip Code   _____ **5.** City   _____ **6.** Telephone Number

2. Work with a partner.

Ask your partner questions about the application.

A What's her address?
B 11 Main Street.

Unit 1

3

1. Practice the dialog.

2. Circle.

Circle Name **and** NAME. **Say the words.**

Employee Information Form

(Name:) **Ana   Torres**
        First Name   Last Name

Application for Employment

LAST NAME: **Torres**

FIRST NAME: **Ana**

3. Write.

Write your name.

Name: _____   _____
            First   Last

Name: _____   _____
            First   Last

4. Listen.

Circle the word you hear.

a.   first   (last)   b.   name   first

c.   first   last   d.   last   first

5. Write.

Write the letter. Say the letter. Say the words.

N n

N n

___N___ ame   _____ ame   _____ ame   _____ ame

___n___ ame   _____ ame   _____ ame   _____ ame

6. Write.

Write your name.

Employee Information Form

Name: _____   _____

First Name   Last Name

Application for Work

_____   _____

Last Name   First Name

1. Practice the dialog.

2. Write.

Write your address.

Address: _____
          Number   Street

Address: _____
          Number   Street

 3. Listen.

Circle the word you hear.

a. (address)   name   number

b. name   street   number

c. address   street   name

d. address   street   number

                              Unit 1

4. Circle.

Circle Address, Number, **and** Street. **Say the words.**

Workforce Program Registration

Name __Baker_____ __Rosa_____
         Last   First

(Address) __15_____ __School Street_____
              Number   Street

5. Write.

Write the letter. Say the letter. Say the words.

A a

A a

__A__DDRESS   ____DDRESS   N __A__ ME   N ____ ME

__a__ ddress   ____ ddress   n __a__ me   n ____ me

6. Write.

Write and say your name and address.

Middleville Vocational Center

_____ _____
First Name   Last Name

_____
Address (Number and Street)

1. Practice the dialog.

A What's your address?
B My address is 26 Bell Street.
A City and state?
B Dallas, Texas.
A What's the zip code?
B 75206.

2. Write.

Write your city, state, and zip code.

City	State	Zip Code
City	State	Zip Code

3. Listen.

Circle the words you hear.

a.   city   (state)   zip code

b.   city   state   zip code

c.   city   state   zip code

4. Circle.

Circle City, State, **and** Zip Code. **Say the words.**

Address: _____8_____Low Street_____
              Number   Street

Los Angeles   California   90025
  (City)   State   Zip Code

5. Write.

Write the letter. Say the letter. Say the words.

C c

C c

___C__ity   __c__ity   Zip ___C__ode   zip __c__ode

_____ity   _____ity   Zip _____ode   zip _____ode

_____ity   _____ity   Zip _____ode   zip _____ode

_____ity   _____ity   Zip _____ode   zip _____ode

6. Write.

Address:_____
              Number   Street

_____
    City   State   Zip Code

Telephone Number

1. Practice the dialog.

A What's your telephone number?
B 703-555-2486.
A 703-555-2486?
B Yes.

2. Write your telephone number.

Telephone Number: _____

Telephone Number: _____

3. Listen.

Do you hear telephone number? **Circle** yes **or** no.

a. (yes)   no   b.   yes   no

c.   yes   no   d.   yes   no

e.   yes   no   f.   yes   no

4. Write.

Write the letter. Say the letter.

T t

T t

5. Circle.

Circle TELEPHONE **and** Telephone. **Say the words.**

GULF TELEPHONE COMPANY

(703) 555-1452

*** Bill Date – May 23 ***

Name & Address   Telephone

A B C D E

 ON YOUR JOB

6. Complete the form.

Name:_____

Telephone Number:_____

Address:_____
              Number   Street

_____
       City   State   Zip Code

Extension

Write the words on the form.

City	Code	Name	Number
State	Street	Telephone	

Application for Employment

First Name _____ Cathy _____   **Last Name** _____ Azizi _____

Address _____ 57 _____   Brown Ave. _____

Los Angeles,   California   90082

Zip

Number _____ 805-555-6552 _____

2. Write.

Write about yourself.

a. My name is _____.

b. My address is _____

_____.

c. My telephone number is _____.

Performance Check

1. Match.

1. _____ name   **a.** 10 Park Street

2. _____ telephone number   **b.** Ana Lee

3. _____ address   **c.** 555-8819

2. Complete the form.

Application for Employment

Name: _____

          First   Last

Telephone Number: _____

Address: _____

         Number   Street

_____

   City   State   Zip Code

Look at the pictures.

Where are the people?

Which places can you name at work?

Getting Started

1. Work with a team.

Match. Say the names of the places.

1

a **SUPPLY ROOM**

2

b **BREAK ROOM**

3

c **LADIES' ROOM**

4

d **OFFICE**

2. Work with a partner.

Point to the pictures. Ask your partner questions.

A Where are they?
B The office.

Unit 2

Places at Work

1. Practice the dialog.

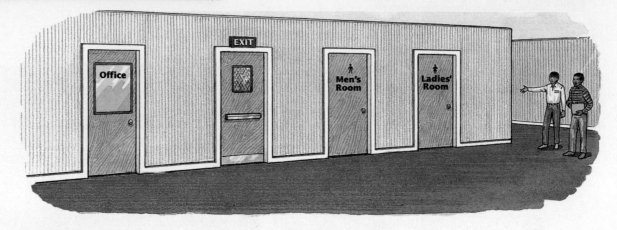

A Excuse me. Where's the exit?
B It's next to the office.
A OK, thanks.

2. Work with a partner.

Circle the words. Say the words.

(men's room)   men's room   exit

ladies' room   ladies' room   office

 3. Listen.

Circle the place you hear.

a. ladies' room   (office)   **b.** break room   ladies' room

c. exit   supply room   **d.** men's room   ladies' room

4. Write.

Write the letters. Say the letters. Say the words.

E e

E e

M m

M m

<u> E </u>xit   <u> e </u>xit   <u> M </u>en's Roo<u> m </u>   <u> m </u>en's roo<u> m </u>

<u>   </u>xit   <u>   </u>xit   <u>   </u>en's Roo<u>   </u>   <u>   </u>en's roo<u>   </u>

<u>   </u>xit   <u>   </u>xit   <u>   </u>en's Roo<u>   </u>   <u>   </u>en's roo<u>   </u>

5. Match.

Look at the picture in 1. Write the letter.

1. **A** Where's the men's room?   **a.** men's room

   B It's next to the <u> c </u>.

2. **A** Where's the exit?   **b.** exit

   B It's next to the <u>   </u>.

3. **A** Where's the office?   **c.** ladies' room

   B It's next to the <u>   </u>.

6. Work with a partner.

Practice the dialogs in 5.

Left   Right

 1. Practice the dialog.

A Where's the supply room?
B It's on the right, next to the exit.
A On the right, next to the exit?
B Yes.
A OK, thanks.

2. Work with a partner.

Circle RIGHT **and** LEFT. **Say the words.**

 KEEP → RIGHT

NO RIGHT TURN ON RED

LEFT TURN ONLY

NO LEFT TURN

 3. Listen.

Circle the word you hear.

a. left (right)   b. left right

c. left right   d. left right

4. Write.

Write the letters. Say the letters. Say the words.

L

L l

R r

R r

__L__adies'   __R__oom ____adies' ____oom ____adies' ____oom

__l__eft   ____eft   ____eft   __r__ight   ____ight   ____ight

supp__l__y   __r__oom supp____y ____oom supp____y ____oom

5. Circle.

Look at the picture in 1. Circle left or right.

1. **A** Where's the supply room?

   B It's on the   left.   (right.)

2. **A** Where's the men's room?

   B It's on the   left.   right.

3. **A** Where's the office?

   B It's on the   left.   right.

6. Work with a partner.

Practice the dialogs in 5.

1. Practice the dialog.

A I need paper.
B Paper's in the supply room.
A Where's the supply room?
B It's on the right.

2. Work with a partner.

Say the words.

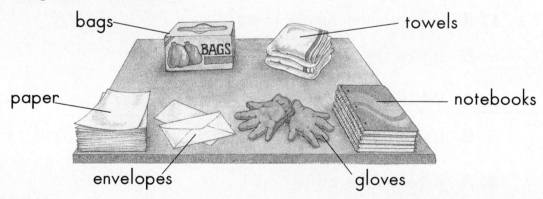

bags
towels
paper
notebooks
envelopes
gloves

3. Listen.

Do you hear supply room? **Circle** yes **or** no.

a. (yes)   no   **b.** yes   no   **c.** yes   no

4. Write.

Write the letter. Say the letter. Say the words.

Ss

Ss

___s__upply   ____upply   ____upply   ____upply   ____upply

5. Check.

Check the supplies you use.
Read the items to a partner.

> **Supplies**
>
> Name: _____
>
> 1. gloves ____   2. paper ✔
> 3. envelopes ____   4. bags ____
> 5. notebooks ____   6. towels ____

6. Match.

What supplies do the people use?
Look at 5. Write the number of the supply.

a. __4__   b. ____   c. ____

1. Practice the dialog.

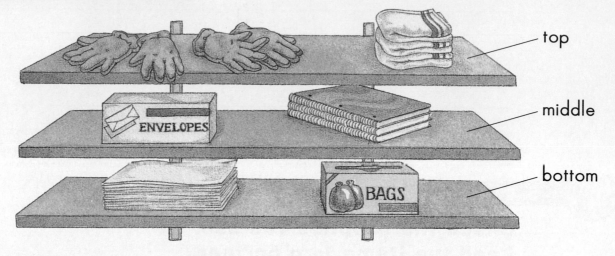

top

middle

bottom

A I need some gloves.
B Gloves are on the top shelf.
A OK.

2. Work with a partner.

Look at 1. What shelf are they on? Say the words.

 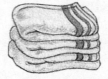 

a. middle   **b.** top   **c.** bottom

 3. Listen.

Look at the picture in 1. Circle yes or no.

a.   yes   (no)   **b.**   yes   no

c.   yes   no   **d.**   yes   no

e.   yes   no   **f.**   yes   no

4. Write.

Write the letters. Say the words.

pape _r_   pape ____   pape ____

_m_ iddl _e_   ____ iddl ____   ____ iddl ____

towe _l_ _s_   towe ____ ____   towe ____ ____

5. Match.

Where are the supplies? Answer the questions.

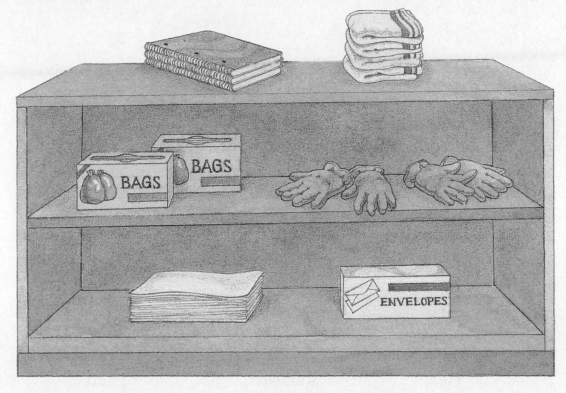

_c_ **1.** Where are the notebooks?   **a.** On the bottom shelf

____ **2.** Where is the paper?   **b.** On the middle shelf

____ **3.** Where are the bags?   **c.** On the top shelf

6. Work with a partner.

Practice the dialogs in 5.

Work with a team.

Count. Write the number of supplies. Circle top, bottom, or middle shelf.

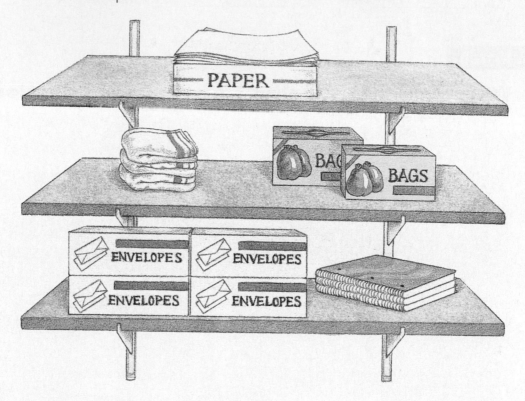

Inventory List

Item	Number		Shelf		
paper	__1__ box		(top)	middle	bottom
bags	____ boxes		top	middle	bottom
notebooks	____		top	middle	bottom
envelopes	____ boxes		top	middle	bottom
towels	____		top	middle	bottom

Performance Check

1. Match.

Write the letter.

a. break room	b. men's room
c. office	d. supply room

2. Circle.

Circle left or right.

a. The ladies' room is on the   left.   right.

b. The men's room is on the   left.   right.

Unit 2

UNIT ◇3◇ Technology

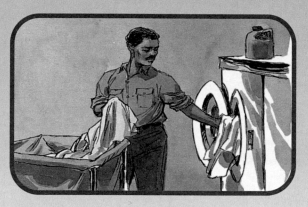

Look at the pictures.

Can you name these machines?

Can you use these machines?

Getting Started

Name the machines. Circle on or off.

vacuum cleaner

(on)   off

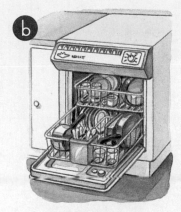

dishwasher

on   off

copier

on   off

coffee maker

on   off

dryer

on   off

microwave oven

on   off

2. Work with a partner.

Point to the pictures. Ask your partner questions.

A Is the vacuum cleaner on?
B Yes,

Push   Pull

1. Practice the dialog.

A Which button do I push?
B Push the green button.
A OK, thanks.

2. Work with a partner.

Say the words.

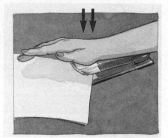

a. push   **b.** pull   **c.** push

 ## 3. Listen.

Circle the word you hear.

a.   push   (pull)   b.   push   pull

c.   push   pull   d.   push   pull

e.   push   pull   f.   push   pull

4. Write.

Write the letter. Say the letter. Say the words.

P p

P p

__P__USH   ____USH   ____USH   ____USH

__p__ull   ____ull   ____ull   ____ull

o__p__en   o____en   o____en   o____en

co__p__ier   co____ier   co____ier   co____ier

5. Circle.

Circle yes **or** no.

a. Push it.   Yes   (No)

b. Pull it.   Yes   No

c. Push her.   Yes   No

d. Pull it.   Yes   No

1. Practice the dialog.

A How do I turn on the microwave oven?

B Push START.

A OK.

B Push STOP to turn off the microwave oven.

A Oh, thanks.

2. Work with a partner.

Circle the word. Say the word.

a. (on)   off   **b.** START   STOP   **c.** start   stop

3. Listen.

Circle the word you hear.

a. (on)   off   **b.** on   off

c. start   stop   **d.** start   stop

e. start   stop   **f.** on   off

4. Write.

Write the letters. Say the letters. Say the words.

O o

O o

S s

S s

O FF	____ FF	____ FF	____ FF
o pen	____ pen	____ pen	____ pen
S TART	____ TART	____ TART	____ TART
s top	____ top	____ top	____ op

5. Write.

Complete the dialogs. Write STOP **or** START.

A How do I turn on the coffee maker?

B Push _____.

A How do I turn off the microwave oven?

B Push _____.

6. Work with a partner.

Practice the dialogs in 5.

1. Practice the dialog.

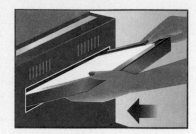

A The copier needs paper. What do I do?
B Oh, take out the tray.
A Yes.
B Put paper in the tray.
A OK.
B Now put the tray in the copier.

2. Work with a partner.

Circle the words. Say the words.

a. put in   take out   **b.** put in   take out

3. Listen.

Circle the words you hear.

a. put in   (take out)   **b.** put in   take out

c. put in   take out   **d.** put in   take out

e. put in   take out   **f.** put in   take out

4. Circle.

Circle Put in **and** take out. **Say the words.**

To Operate:

1. (Put in) the clothes.
2. Put in the soap.
3. Push START.
4. When the machine stops, take out the clothes promptly.

5. Work with a partner.

Match. Say the sentences.

a. Put in water.   b. Turn on the machine.

c. Take out the old filter.   d. Put in the coffee.

e. Put in a new filter.   f. Push START.

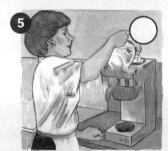

Unit 3

Open   Close

1. Practice the dialog.

A How do I use the copier?

B Well, open the top.

A Do I put the paper here?

B Yes, now close the top. Push START.

A OK.

B Your copy comes out here.

2. Work with a partner.

Circle the word. Say the word.

a. (open) close   **b.** open close   **c.** open close   **d.** open close

 3. Listen.

Circle the word you hear.

a. open (close)   **b.** open   close

c. open   close   **d.** open   close

34   Unit 3

4. Write.

Write the letter. Say the letter. Say the words.

U u

U u

vac__u__ __u__m   vac____ ____m   vac____ ____m   vac____ ____m

p__u__sh   p____sh   p____sh   p____sh

p__u__ll   p____ll   p____ll   p____ll

o__u__t   o____t   o____t   o____t

5. Circle.

Circle OPEN and CLOSE. Say the words.

Extension

1. Work with a partner.

Look at the pictures. Circle the words you see.

READY TO MAKE COPIES

(ON   OFF)

START   STOP

ON   OFF

START   STOP

ON   OFF

START   STOP

2. Write.

Write the machines you can use.

coffee maker	copier	dishwasher	dryer
microwave oven	vacuum cleaner	washing machine	

I can use a _____

_____.

3. Work with a partner.

Look at 2. Tell your partner the machines you can use.

Unit 3

Performance Check

1. Match.

a. ON   b. OFF   c. START   d. STOP

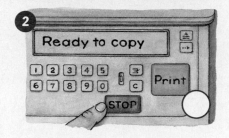

2. Circle.

Read the directions. Circle yes **or** no.

To Operate the Dishwasher:
1. **Open the door.**
2. **Put dishes in the trays.**
3. **Add soap.**
4. **Close the door.**
5. **Push START.**

a. Put soap in the trays.   yes   no

b. Push STOP to turn on the machine.   yes   no

c. Push START to turn on the machine.   yes   no

Time Management

Look at the pictures.

Can you say the times?

Can you say the dates?

Getting Started

1. Work with a team.

Circle the dates and times. Say the dates and times.

a March

S	M	T	W	T	F	S
	1	2	3	4	5	6
7	8	9	10	11	12	13
14	15	16	17	18	19	20
21	22	23	24	25	26	27
28	29	30	31			

March 2
(March 14)

b August

S	M	T	W	T	F	S
1	2	3	4	5	6	7
8	9	10	11	12	13	14
15	16	17	18	19	20	21
22	23	24	25	26	27	28
29	30	31				

August 2
August 8

c September

S	M	T	W	T	F	S
				1	2	3	4
5	6	7	8	9	10	11
12	13	14	15	16	17	18
19	20	21	22	23	24	25
26	27	28	29	30		

September 9
September 17

12:00
2:00

6:10
10:30

9:45
8:00

2. Work with a partner.

Point to the pictures. Ask your partner questions.

A What's the date?
B March 14,

A What time is it?
B 2:00.

Days of the Week

1. Practice the dialog.

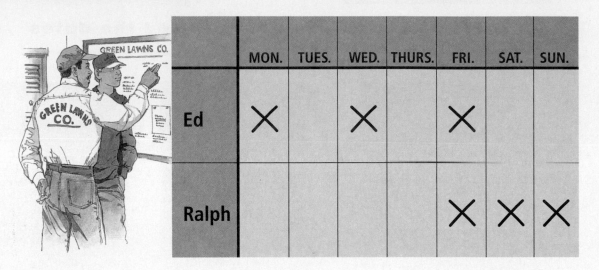

	MON.	TUES.	WED.	THURS.	FRI.	SAT.	SUN.
Ed	X		X		X		
Ralph					X	X	X

A What days do you work, Ed?
B Monday, Wednesday, and Friday. How about you, Ralph?
A Friday, Saturday, and Sunday.
B Great, I'll see you on Friday.

2. Work with a partner.

Circle the days. Say the days.

Work Schedule: Week of July 10 - July 16

(Sunday)	Monday	Tuesday	Wednesday	Thursday	Friday	Saturday
	9-5	9-1		10-2	11-3	12-6

3. Listen.

Circle the day you hear.

a. Monday   (Thursday)   **b.** Tuesday   Friday

c. Saturday   Sunday   **d.** Thursday   Tuesday

4. Write.

Write the letters. Say the letters. Say the words.

D d

D d

W w

W w

Sun__d__ay   Sun____ay   Sun____ay

Mon__d__ay   Mon____ay   Mon____ay

Fri__d__ay   Fri____ay   Fri____ay

Satur__d__ay   Satur____ay   Satur____ay

__W__e__d__nes__d__ay   ____e____nes____ay   ____e____nes____ay

Thurs__d__ay   Thurs____ay   Thurs____ay

5. Circle.

Circle the days you go to class. Tell your partner.

Sunday   Monday   Tuesday   Wednesday

Thursday   Friday   Saturday

6. Circle.

Circle the days you work. Tell your partner.

Sunday   Monday   Tuesday   Wednesday

Thursday   Friday   Saturday

1. Practice the dialog.

March						
S	**M**	**T**	**W**	**T**	**F**	**S**
	1	2	3	4	5	6
7	8	9	10	(11)	12	13
14	15	16	17	18	19	20
21	22	23	24	25	26	27
28	29	30	31			

A What's today's date?
B Thursday, March 11.
A Oh, good. Tomorrow's Friday.

2. Repeat.

**Your teacher says the numbers.
You say the numbers.**

1st	10th	20th	27th
2nd	11th	21st	28th
3rd	12th	22nd	29th
4th	13th	23rd	30th
5th	14th	24th	31st

3. Listen.

Circle the date you hear.

a.	November 8	November 9	(November 10)
b.	December 12	December 13	December 30
c.	June 25	June 26	June 27
d.	July 4	July 14	July 20

4. Write.

Write the letter. Say the letter. Say the words.

J j

J j

____January   ____anuary   ____anuary   ____anuary

____June   ____une   ____une   ____une

____July   ____uly   ____uly   ____uly

5. Circle.

Circle the dates. Say the dates.

Work Schedule: (November 12) - November 16

	Monday	Tuesday	Wednesday	Thursday	Friday
Mark	✓	✓	✓	✓	✓
Theresa	✓		✓		✓

Invoice #3209   Date: August 8
Sold to: Alan Martin

Quantity	Item	Unit	Cost
40 boxes	envelopes	$2.75	$110.00

6. Work with a partner.

Ask your partner. Write the answers.

a. What's today's date? _____

b. What's tomorrow's date? _____

1. Practice the dialog.

January	February	March	April
May	June	July	August
September	October	November	December

A What's your date of birth?
B January 7, 1984.
A Excuse me? What year?
B 1984.

2. Work with a partner.

Circle month **and** year. **Circle the dates.**
Say the dates.

Driver's License

Name: Luis Santos
Date of Birth:
July 10, 1957
(month)/day/year

Driver's License

Name: Elena Peters
Date of Birth:
April 5, 1943
month/day/year

3. Listen.

Circle the year you hear.

a. 1977   1987   (1997)   b. 1979   1989   2009

c. 1994   1999   2001   d. 1982   1989   1992

4. Write.

Write the letters. Say the letters. Say the words.

V v

V v

Y y

Y y

No__v__ember   No_____ember   __y__ear   _____ear

Jul__y__   Jul_____   Ma__y__   Ma_____

5. Read. Write today's date.

January 7, 1984
Date of Birth

Melissa Hicks
Signature   Date

 **6. Write.**

Complete the form. Write about yourself.

Date of Birth

Signature   Date

Unit 4   45

Time

1. Practice the dialog.

A What time is it?
B It's 1:30.
A Excuse me? 1:30?
B Yes, that's right.

2. Work with a partner.

Say the times.

a. It's 9:00.

b. It's 3:15.

c. It's 2:30.

d. It's 7:45.

e. It's 5:10.

f. It's 11:40.

Unit 4

3. Listen.

Circle the time you hear.

a. (4:00)   5:00   8:00   b.   5:30   6:30   7:30

c.   11:15   12:15   4:15   d.   5:45   7:45   9:45

4. Circle.

Circle the times. Say the times.

Time Card

Name:	Wanda Chin		Employee #: 3228
Date	Time In		Time Out
April 2	(7:22)		3:35
April 3	7:31		3:30

5. Write.

Write the times.
Ask and say the times with your partner.

a. ___4:15___   b. _____   c. _____

6. Ask your partner the time.

1. Make a schedule for the week.

Write the times you go to class.
Write the times you go to work.

Sunday	_____
	_____
Monday	_____
	_____
Tuesday	_____
	_____
Wednesday	_____
	_____
Thursday	_____
	_____
Friday	_____
	_____
Saturday	_____

2. Write.

Answer the questions.

a. What days do you go to class?

_____

b. What time do you go to work?

_____

Performance Check

1. Circle the days. Underline the months.

Friday	May	Wednesday	September
October	Tuesday	August	Thursday
Sunday	December	March	February
January	Saturday	Monday	July

2. Write the dates and the times.

June 1999	April 1996	July 2001
S M T W T F S	S M T W T F S	S M T W T F S

June 1999

S	M	T	W	T	F	S
		1	2	3	4	5
6	7	8	9	(10)	11	12
13	14	15	16	17	18	19
20	21	22	23	24	25	26
27	28	29	21	30		

April 1996

S	M	T	W	T	F	S
	1	2	3	4	5	6
7	8	9	10	11	12	13
14	15	16	17	18	19	20
21	22	(23)	24	25	26	27
28	29	30				

July 2001

S	M	T	W	T	F	S
1	2	3	4	(5)	6	7
8	9	10	11	12	13	14
15	16	17	18	19	20	21
22	23	24	25	26	27	28
29	30	31				

a. _____   b. _____   c. _____

d. _____   e. _____   f. _____

3. Write your date of birth.

_____

Unit 4

49

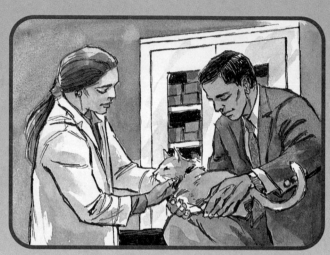

Look at the pictures.

Who are the workers?

Who are the customers?

Are the workers doing a
good job?

Getting Started

Are the workers doing a good job? Circle yes **or** no.

a. (yes) no

b. yes no

c. yes no

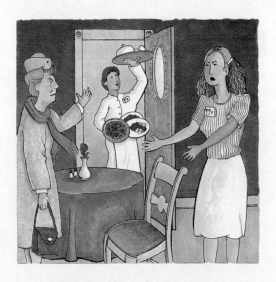

d. yes no

2. Work with a partner.

Point to the pictures. Ask your partner questions.

A Is he doing a good job?
B Yes.

Unit 5

1. Practice the dialog.

A May I help you?
B Yes, coffee, please.
A Here you are.
B Thank you.
A You're welcome.

2. Work with a partner.

Circle please **and** thank you. **Say the words.**

Coffee, please.

Thank you.

3. Listen.

Circle the words you hear.

a. (please) thank you   **b.** please   thank you

c. please   thank you   **d.** please   thank you

4. Circle.

Circle Please **and** Thank you.

(Please) wait in line.

Thank you. Please come again.

Please have ID ready.

Thank you for not smoking.

5. Write.

Write please **or** Thank you.

A Ten stamps, _____.

B Here you are.

A _____

6. Work with a partner.

Practice the dialog in 5.

1. Practice the dialog.

A Hello, may I help you?
B Yes, this telephone doesn't work.
A OK, please take it to Customer Service.
B Thank you.

2. Work with a partner.

Circle the picture. Say the words.

a. Hello

b. Customer Service

3. Listen.

Do you hear Customer Service? **Circle** yes **or** no.

a. (yes) no   b.   yes   no

c.   yes   no   d.   yes   no

4. Write.

Write the letters. Say the letters. Say the words.

H h

H h

I i

I i

h ello   ____ ello   serv i ce   serv ____ ce
h ello   ____ ello   serv i ce   serv ____ ce

5. Circle.

Circle Customer Service. **Say the words.**

Customer Service

Gift Wrap
Layaway
Returns and Exchanges

Hours: 10:00 – 8:00

Store Directory

↑ **Children's Clothes**
→ **Customer Service**
↤ **Ladies' Clothes**
↓ **Men's Clothes**

Unit 5   55

1. Practice the dialog.

A Excuse me. I think this price is wrong.
B You're right. I'm sorry. Let me fix the mistake.
A Good. I'll take it.
B Thank you. Goodbye.
A Goodbye.

2. Work with a partner.

Circle the words. Say the words.

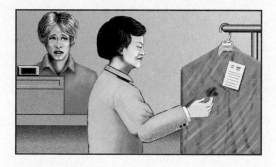   

a.   Sorry   Goodbye   **b.**   Sorry   Goodbye

 3. Listen.

Circle the word you hear.

a. (sorry)   goodbye   **b.**   sorry   goodbye

c.   sorry   goodbye   **d.**   sorry   goodbye

Write the letter. Say the letter. Say the words.

G g

G g

__G_OODBYE   ____OODBYE   _G_OOD   ____OOD

__g_oodbye   ____oodbye   _g_ood   ____ood

__g_oodbye   ____oodbye   _g_ood   ____ood

5. Circle.

Circle Sorry **and** Goodbye. **Say the words.**

6. Match.

Write the letter. Practice the dialog with a partner.

A __d__ , may I help you?

B I think the price is wrong on these towels.

A Oh, I'm ____. You're right. I'll fix it.

B ____ you. Goodbye.

A ____

a. sorry

b. Goodbye.

c. Thank

d. Hello

1. Practice the dialog.

A Hello, may I help you?

B This battery doesn't work.

A I'm sorry. Do you want an exchange or a refund?

B A refund, please.

A OK, please fill out the form.

B Thank you.

2. Work with a partner.

Circle Exchange, exchange, Refund, **and** refund.
Say the words.

(Exchange) and
Refund Policy

Please keep this receipt
for exchange or refund.

3. Listen.

Circle the word you hear.

a.   exchange   (refund)   **b.**   exchange   refund

c.   exchange   refund   **d.**   exchange   refund

Write the letters. Say the letters. Say the words.

Xx

Xx

Ff

Ff

E__X__CHANGE   E____CHANGE   O__F__ __F__   O____ ____

e__x__change   e____change   e__x__it   e____it

co__f__ __f__ee   co____ ____ee   re__f__und   re____und

5. Write.

Get a refund. Complete the refund form.

Customer Name:_____ Date:_____

Address:_____

City:_____ State:_____ Zip Code:_____

Telephone Number:_____

Item: _Dryer_____

Date of Purchase: _May 20_____

Mark (X) one: Exchange ( ) Refund (X)

Amount: _$250.00_____

Extension

Write.

The microwave oven doesn't work. Get a refund. Complete the form. Use the receipt.

HOME STORE

Microwave oven	$75.00
Total	**$75.00**

March 5   16:43

HOME STORE
RETURN REQUEST FORM

Date:_____

Customer Name:_____

Address:_____

City:_____ State:_____ Zip Code:_____

Telephone Number: _____

Item: Microwave oven_____

Date of Purchase:_____

Exchange ( ) Refund ( )

Amount:_____

Performance Check

1. Match.

a. Hello.   b. I'm sorry.   c. Goodbye.

2. Complete the dialog.

Customer   Please   you

A Excuse me. This microwave oven doesn't work.

B Oh, I'm sorry. _____ take it to

_____ Service. It's next to the exit.

A Thank _____.

3. Circle the word.

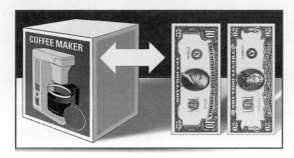 

a.   refund   exchange   b.   refund   exchange

Look at the pictures.

Where are the people?

What are they doing?

Getting Started

1. Work with a team.

Match. Say the words.

a. Be on time.   b. Be careful.
c. Call in.   d. Punch in. Punch out.

2. Work with a partner.

Point to the pictures.
Your partner says what to do.

A Punch in. Punch out.

1. Practice the dialog.

A Hello, Ms. Brown. It's Luz.
B Hello, Luz.
A I'm sorry. I'm going to be late. My son is sick.
B All right, Luz. Thanks for calling.

2. Work with a partner.

Work starts at 9:00. Say the words.

a. early   **b.** on time   **c.** late

3. Listen.

Circle the words you hear.

a.   on time   (early)   late   **b.**   on time   early   late

c.   on time   early   late   **d.**   on time   early   late

4. Write.

Write the words. Say the words.

on time _____ _____

late _____ _____

early _____ _____

5. Write.

Work starts at 8:30.
Write late, early, **or** on time. **Say the words.**

a. ___on time___   b. _____   c. _____

6. Write.

Write the time. Write on time, late, **or** early.

I start work at _____.   I start work _____.

7. Write.

You're late for class or work. Who do you call?
Write the name and number.

Name: _____

Telephone number: _____

Understand   Repeat

 1. Practice the dialog.

A Please take the TVs to the supply room.
B I'm sorry. I don't understand. Can you repeat that?
A Take the TVs to the supply room.
B Oh, OK.

2. Write.

Write the words. Say the words.

I don't __understand__ .   I don't _____ .

I don't _____ .   I don't _____ .

Can you __repeat__ that?   Can you _____ that?

Can you _____ that?   Can you _____ that?

 3. Listen.

Do you hear repeat? Circle yes or no.

a. (yes) no   **b.** yes no

c. yes no   **d.** yes no

e. yes no   **f.** yes no

4. Write.

Write understand **or** repeat.

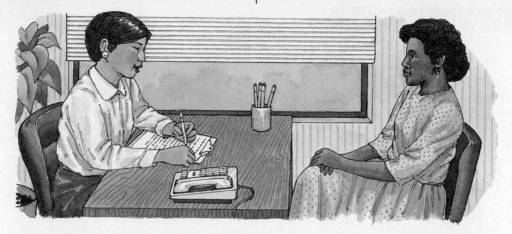

A What's your telephone number?

B 555-3498.

A I'm sorry. Can you _____ that?

B 555-3498.

A Thank you.

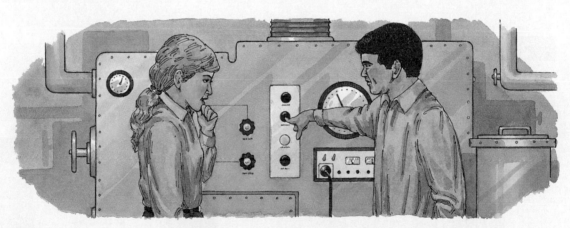

A Can you help me?

B Sure, what's the matter?

A I don't _____ how to use this machine.

B I'll help you.

A Thank you.

5. Work with a partner.

Practice the dialogs in 4.

Unit 6

1. Practice the dialog.

A Monica! Be careful! Put on your goggles!
B Oh, I'm sorry.

2. Work with a partner.

Circle CAREFUL, careful, quiet **and** QUIET.
Say the words.

WET FLOOR.

BE CAREFUL.

Testing:
Please
be quiet.

Be careful.
Wet paint.

BE QUIET

3. Write.

Write the letters. Say the letters. Say the words.

Q q

Q q

Z z

Z z

_Q_UIET   _____UIET   _q_uiet   _____uiet

_Z_ONE   _____ONE   _z_one   _____one

_q_uiet   _____uiet   _z_one   _____one

4. Write.

Write the words. Say the words.

careful   Zone

a. Work _____

b. Be _____ .

Unit 6

1. Practice the dialog.

A George, do you take the bus to work?
B Yes, I take the 57 bus.

2. Work with a partner.

Circle WALK, drive, **and** Take. **Say the words.**

DON'T
WALK

Take the Train
15 minutes to
downtown

Please
drive
carefully.

3. Listen.

Circle the word you hear.

a.	walk	drive	(take)	**b.**	walk	drive	take
c.	walk	drive	take	**d.**	walk	drive	take
e.	walk	drive	take	**f.**	walk	drive	take

4. Write.

Write the letters. Say the letters. Say the words.

K k

K k

B b

B b

WAL __K__   WAL _____   __B__ US   _____ US

__w__ alk   _____ alk   __b__ us   _____ us

5. Work with a partner.

How do they go to work? Match.

a. They drive.   b. They take the bus.   c. They walk.

6. Write.

Write walk, drive, **or** take the bus.

I _____ to work.

Read and write.

Write early **or** late.

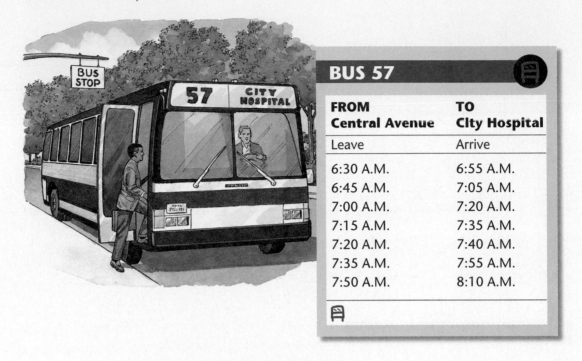

BUS 57	
FROM **Central Avenue**	**TO** **City Hospital**
Leave	Arrive
6:30 A.M.	6:55 A.M.
6:45 A.M.	7:05 A.M.
7:00 A.M.	7:20 A.M.
7:15 A.M.	7:35 A.M.
7:20 A.M.	7:40 A.M.
7:35 A.M.	7:55 A.M.
7:50 A.M.	8:10 A.M.

First shift at City Hospital starts at 7:30.

a. Pablo is taking the bus at 7:00.

He's going to be ___early___ for work.

b. Amy is taking the bus at 7:20.

She's going to be _____ for work.

c. Stan is taking the bus at 6:45.

He's going to be _____ for work.

d. Ji Sun is taking the bus at 7:15.

She's going to be _____ for work.

Performance Check

1. Write.

Work starts at 8:00. Write on time, late, **or** early.

a. _____ b. _____ c. _____

2. Match.

a. Work Zone   b. Be quiet.   c. Be careful.

3. Write.

How do you go to work or school?
Write walk, drive **or** take the bus.

I _____.

Look at the pictures.

Where are the people?

What are they doing?

Getting Started

1. Work with a team.

Match. Say the words.

1 e

2 ○

3 ○

4 ○

5  ○

6  ○

7  ○

8  ○

a. ten dollars

b. a dime
ten cents

c. a dollar

d. a quarter
twenty-five cents

e. a penny
one cent

f. five dollars

g. twenty dollars

h. a nickel
five cents

2. Work with a partner.

Point to the pictures. Ask your partner questions.

A How much is it?
B One cent.

Unit 7

1. Practice the dialog.

A That's $22.50, please.
B Here's $30.00.
A Your change is $7.50.
B Thank you.

2. Work with a partner.

Circle the prices. Say the prices.

$1.75 ○   **$11.50** ○   **$99.95** ○

3. Listen.

Circle the amount you hear.

a.	$21.09	($21.90)	b.	$15.10	$15.11
c.	$13.60	$13.70	d.	$7.14	$7.40
e.	$.65	$65.00	f.	$32.88	$32.89

4. Write.

Write the amounts. Say the amounts.

a. ___$12.35___

_____

b. _____

_____

c. _____

_____

5. Work with a partner.

Write the change.

○ **$12.00**

○ **$1.25**

○ **$10.50**

a. ___$3.00___

_____

b. _____

_____

c. _____

_____

6. Work with a partner.

Practice the dialog. Use the prices from 5.

A That's ___$12.00___, please.

B Here's ___$15.00___

A Your change is ___$3.00___.

B Thank you.

Cash   Check

1. Practice the dialogs.

A That's $32.50.
Cash or check?

B Check.

A I need your driver's
license, please.

B OK, here.

A That's $11.00.
Cash or check?

B Cash.

A OK, thank you.

2. Work with a partner.

Look at the check. Circle yes **or** no.

Ana Santos   581
12 Bay Drive
Long Beach, CA   DATE _January 31, 1999_

PAY TO THE
ORDER OF ___Northland Hardware___ $ 32.50

Thirty-two and 50/100 _____ DOLLARS

※ **CAL**BANK   _Ana Santos_

---

a. The check is for $50.00.   yes   (no)

b. The check is to Northland Hardware.   yes   no

c. The check is from Ana Santos.   yes   no

3. Listen.

Write cash **or** check.

a. _____cash_____   b. _____

c. _____   d. _____

4. Match.

Match the amounts.

__c__ **1.** $15.95   **a.** Twenty-one and 50/100 DOLLARS

____ **2.** $21.50   **b.** Sixty-two and 75/100 DOLLARS

____ **3.** $62.75   **c.** Fifteen and 95/100 DOLLARS

5. Write.

Write the amounts for checks.

$40.20 _____Forty and 20/100_____ Dollars

$71.05 _____ Dollars

$65.30 _____ Dollars

6. Write.

Write a check to Northland Hardware for $34.78.

```
                                         226

                        DATE _____

PAY TO THE
ORDER OF _____  $ [_____]

_____  _____ DOLLARS


✳ CALBANK          ____  ____  ____  ____
```

Unit 7

1. Practice the dialog.

ENDORSE HERE

Hector Perez

_____

_____

DO NOT WRITE OR SIGN BELOW THIS LINE

A Hello, I want to cash my paycheck.
B I need some ID, please.
A Here's my driver's license.
B Thank you. Sign your name here.

2. Work with a partner.

What is it? Circle the words. Say the words.

Green Tree Co.   48295
23 South Street
Boston, MA 02111

Pay to the
order of ___Arturo Morales_____ $ 400.00
Four hundred and no/100 dollars_____

                         Bill Perkins

Driver's License

12897654
Arturo Morales
12 Third Street
Boston, MA 02125

DOB: 05-05-58

a.   paycheck   ID   **b.**   cash   ID

Do they ask for ID? Circle yes **or** no.

a. (yes)   no   b.   yes   no

c.   yes   no   d.   yes   no

4. Read and write.

Read the paycheck. Write the answers.

Medical Labs	DATE June 1, 2000
44 Sky Avenue	
Chicago, IL 60609	

PAY TO THE ORDER OF _____ MEI CHIN _____

THREE HUNDRED TWENTY-FIVE AND 14/100 DOLLARS _____ $ | 325.14 |

✦**National** Bank   *Ellen Martinka*

a. Who is the check for? _____ Mei Chin _____

b. What is the amount of the check? _____

c. What is the date of the check? _____

5. Write.

Sign the backs of the checks.

ENDORSE HERE	ENDORSE HERE
_____	_____
_____	_____
DO NOT WRITE OR SIGN BELOW THIS LINE	DO NOT WRITE OR SIGN BELOW THIS LINE

Deposit

1. Practice the dialog.

A Hello, I want to deposit this check.
B OK, please fill out a deposit slip.
A Thank you.

2. Circle.

Circle DEPOSIT. **Circle** yes **or** no.

DEPOSIT TICKET	Cash	
Name Eric Waters	Checks	$257.28
Date July 6 19 99		
▰▰ SOUTH SIDE BANK	Total	$257.28

a. Eric is depositing his check. (yes) no

b. The check is for $275.80. yes no

c. The date is July 6. yes no

d. Eric's bank is North Bank. yes no

3. Listen.

Do you hear deposit? **Circle** yes **or** no.

a. (yes)   no   **b.** yes   no

c. yes   no   **d.** yes   no

e. yes   no   **f.** yes   no

4. Write.

You have a check for $251.77. Deposit it.

DEPOSIT TICKET		
	CASH	
Name_____	CHECKS	
Address_____		
_____		
Date_____		
_____		
SIGN HERE		
✶*Trust Bank*	TOTAL	

5. Write.

You have a check for $361.21. Deposit it.

DEPOSIT TICKET		
	CASH	
Name_____	CHECKS	
Address_____		
_____		
Date_____		
SIGN HERE		
	TOTAL	

Extension

1. Circle.

Circle the item you want.

Dart Discount

Vacuum Cleaner $112.99

Television $129.99

Telephone $32.95

Camera $89.90

Personal Radio $12.45

Lamp $19.50

Washer $199.95

2. Write.

Buy the item. Write a check.

```
                                                    227

                          DATE _____

PAY TO THE
ORDER OF_____  $ [        ]

_____  DOLLARS


✳ CALBANK          _____
```

84

Unit 7

1. Write.

Write the amounts.

a. _____   b. _____   c. _____

2. Write.

Write a check to Green's Grocery for $40.82.

	375
	DATE _____
PAY TO THE ORDER OF _____	$ [_____]
_____ DOLLARS	
✳ **CAL**BANK	_____

3. Listen.

Circle the amount you hear.

a.	$27.98	$27.99	b.	$14.80	$48.00
c.	$14.01	$111.10	d.	$15.55	$55.15
e.	$30.25	$30.52	f.	$11.11	$1.11

UNIT 8 Health and Safety

DANGER
SAFETY GLASSES
REQUIRED

POISON

FIRST STREET BAKERY

TELEPHONE   TELE

Look at the pictures.

Where are the people?

What are they doing?

Getting Started

1. Work with a team.

Match. Write the letter.

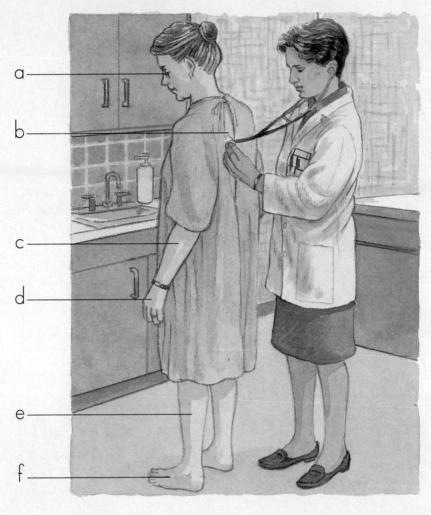

1. __c__ arm   2. ____ foot

3. ____ back   4. ____ hand

5. ____ leg   6. ____ eye

2. Work with a partner.

**Give your partner instructions.
Your partner points to the picture.**

A Point to her arm.

Unit 8

87

Hurt   Cut   Broken

 1. Practice the dialog.

A What's the matter?
B My arm is hurt.

2. Work with a partner.

Write the words. Say the words.

a. cut

b. hurt

c. broken

_____   _____   _____

 3. Listen.

Circle the word you hear.

a. cut   (hurt)   **b.**   cut   broken

c. broken   hurt   **d.**   hurt   cut

4. Write.

Complete the sentences.

broken	cut	hurt	hurt

a. His back is ___hurt___.

b. Her arm is _____.

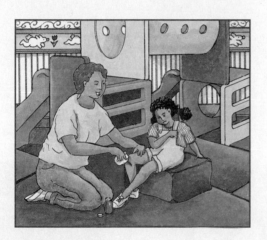

c. Her leg is _____.

d. His foot is _____.

5. Write.

You're hurt. Complete the dialog.

A What's the matter?

B My _____ is _____.

6. Work with a partner.

Practice the dialog in 5.

Unit 8

1. Practice the dialog.

A Be careful!
B What's the matter?
A Look at the sign. No smoking.

2. Work with a partner.

Say the words.

a. DANGER   **b.** NO SMOKING   **c.** POISON

3. Listen.

Circle the words you hear.

a.	(no smoking) danger		**b.**	poison no smoking
c.	poison danger		**d.**	no smoking poison
e.	danger poison		**f.**	danger no smoking

Circle DANGER, NO SMOKING, **and** POISON.
Say the words.

Are they following the signs? Circle yes or no.

a. yes no   **b.** yes   no

c. yes   no   **d.** yes   no

1. Practice the dialog.

A Park City 911. What's the emergency?
B There's a fire.
A Where?
B 38 Green Street.
A OK, we'll send help right away.

2. Work with a partner.

Circle FIRE, ACCIDENT, Fire, **and** 911.
Say the words.

Let's Be
ACCIDENT
FREE

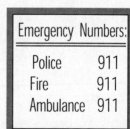

Emergency Numbers:	
Police	911
Fire	911
Ambulance	911

3. Listen.

Circle the word you hear.

a.   accident   (fire)   **b.**   accident   fire

c.   accident   fire   **d.**   accident   fire

e.   accident   fire   **f.**   accident   fire

4. Write.

**Write the words and numbers.
Say the words and numbers.**

fire	_____	_____
fire	_____	_____
accident	_____	_____
911	_____	_____

5. Work with a partner.

**Where's the fire? Where's the accident?
Write the addresses.**

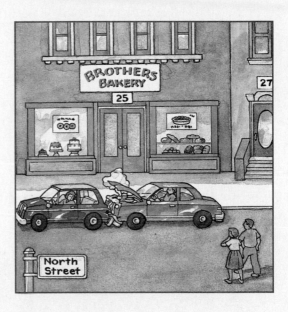

a.  73 Bank Street

b. _____

6. Work with a partner.

Practice calling 911. Use the places in 5.

A Hope Town 911. What's the emergency?

B There's a _____ fire _____

A Where?

B _____

A OK, we'll send help right away.

Unit 8

1. Practice the dialog.

A What's the matter?
B My leg is hurt.
A You need to go to the emergency room.

2. Work with a partner.

Circle Hospital **and** Emergency Room.
Say the words.

GENERAL HOSPITAL

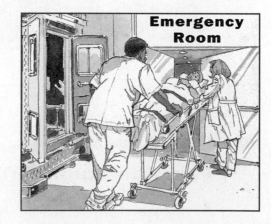

Emergency Room

3. Listen.

What do the people do? Circle.

a. (Go to the hospital.) Call 911.

b. Go to the hospital. Call 911.

c. Go to the hospital. Call 911.

d. Go to the hospital. Call 911.

4. Write.

<u>   hospital   </u>   <u>   </u>   <u>   </u>

<u>emergency room</u>   <u>   </u>   <u>   </u>

5. Work with a partner.

Complete the dialog. Practice the dialog.

cut   emergency   hand   Hospital

A What's the matter?

B My <u> hand </u> is <u>   </u>.

A You need to go to the <u>   </u> room at

City <u>   </u>.

Unit 8

95

Look.

What's missing from the signs? Write the words.

| Danger | Fire | No Smoking | Poison |

a. _____Danger_____

b. _____

c. _____

d. _____ Extinguisher

Performance Check

1. Write the word.

arm   foot   hand   leg

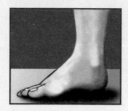

a. _____   b. _____   c. _____   d. _____

2. Write.

Complete the sentences.

fire   hurt

a. Her back is _____.   b. There's a _____.

3. Circle.

Look at the pictures. Circle the words.

a. Danger   No Smoking   b. Poison   Accident

Unit 8

97

Look at the pictures.

What are the people doing?

Do you work with other people?

Who do you work with?

Getting Started

1. Work with a team.

What do they say? Write the letter.

a. Where are you from?   b. Good work.

c. Nice to meet you.   d. I'm sorry.

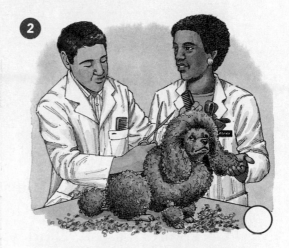

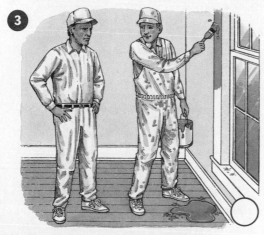

2. Work with a partner.

Point to the pictures. Ask your partner questions.

A What's he saying?
B Nice to meet you.

Unit 9

1. Practice the dialog.

A Van, this is Luis. Luis is your supervisor.
B Hi, Van. Welcome to the team.
C Thanks, Luis. Glad to be here.
B Let's meet your coworkers.
C Great!

2. Work with a partner.

Say the words.

a. coworkers   **b.** supervisor

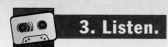

3. Listen.

Circle the word you hear.

a. coworkers (supervisor)   b. coworkers   supervisor

c. coworkers   supervisor   d. coworkers   supervisor

4. Look.

Circle the supervisors.

5. Write.

Write the words. Say the words.

coworkers   _____   _____   _____

coworkers   _____   _____   _____

supervisor   _____   _____   _____

supervisor   _____   _____   _____

6. Write.

Write the names of people from your workplace or class.

Coworkers: _____

Supervisor: _____

Introductions

1. Practice the dialog.

A Hi, I'm Lin.
B Nice to meet you, Lin. I'm Ted.
A Nice to meet you, Ted.
B Where are you from, Lin?
A I'm from Korea. Where are you from?
B I'm from Los Angeles.

2. Match.

What do they say? Write the letter. Say the words.

a. Where are you from?
b. Nice to meet you.

3. Listen.

Do you hear Nice to meet you? **Circle** yes **or** no.

a. (yes)　　no　　　　b.　yes　　no

c.　yes　　no　　　　d.　yes　　no

4. Write.

Write the words. Say the words.

Nice to meet you.　　　　Where are you from?

_____　　_____

_____　　_____

_____　　_____

5. Write.

Complete the dialog.

| from | Hi | meet | Nice | Where |

A _____Hi_____, I'm Anton.

B Nice to _____ you, Anton. I'm Mei.

A _____ to meet you, Mei.

B Where are you _____, Anton?

A I'm from Russia. _____ are you from?

B I'm from China.

6. Work with a partner.

Practice the dialog in 5. Use your own names and countries.

Break   Lunch

1. Practice the dialog.

A Sue, what time is the morning break?
B It's at 10:00.
A And what time is lunch?
B Lunch is at 12:00. Let's eat lunch together.
A OK, I'll see you at 12:00.

2. Work with a partner.

Look at the schedule. Circle the times.

> ### Memorandum
>
> **TO:** All Employees
> **FROM:** Tony Rizzo,
> Warehouse Superintendent
>
> Please follow this schedule for all breaks:
>
> | | |
> |---|---|
> | Morning Break | 10:00 |
> | Lunch | 12:00 |
> | Afternoon Break | 3:00 |

a. What time is the afternoon break?   10:00   12:00   (3:00)

b. What time is the morning break?   10:00   12:00   3:00

c. What time is lunch?   10:00   12:00   3:00

3. Listen.

Circle the words you hear.

a. lunch (afternoon break)   **b.** morning break   lunch

c. lunch   afternoon break   **d.** morning break   lunch

4. Write.

Write the words. Say the words.

<u>break</u>   <u>   </u>   <u>   </u>   <u>   </u>

<u>lunch</u>   <u>   </u>   <u>   </u>   <u>   </u>

5. Write.

Complete the schedule.
Write about your workplace or school.

SCHEDULE

MORNING BREAK _____

LUNCH _____

AFTERNOON BREAK _____

6. Work with a partner.

Ask your partner about his or her schedule.
Write his or her answers. Then practice the dialog.

A What time is your morning break?

B It's at _____

A And what time is lunch?

B Lunch is at _____.

Good work

1. Practice the dialogs.

A These dishes look great. Good work!

B Thank you, Ms. Green.

A That grass doesn't look very good. Please cut it again.

B Oh, I'm sorry. I'll cut it again now.

2. Work with a partner.

Do they say Good work? **Circle** yes **or** no.

a. (yes) no   **b.** yes no   **c.** yes no

Unit 9

3. Listen.

Do you hear Good work? **Circle** yes **or** no.

a. (yes)   no   **b.**   yes   no

c. yes   no   **d.**   yes   no

4. Write.

Write the words. Say the words.

good work   _____   _____

good work   _____   _____

good work   _____   _____

5. Write.

What do they say? Write I'm sorry **or** Thank you.

A These copies look great. Good work!

B _____ , Mr. Hill.

A These towels don't look very good. Please wash them again.

B _____ .
I'll wash them again now.

6. Work with a partner.

Practice the dialogs in 5.

Extension

1. Read.

Read the company rules.

Company Rules

1. Work begins at 8:00 and ends at 5:00.
2. Breaks are at 10:30 and 3:30.
3. Breaks are 15 minutes long.
4. Lunch is from 12:30 to 1:00.
5. Workers need to wear safety glasses.
6. Workers need to wear gloves.

2. Write.

Which rule are they following? Write the number.

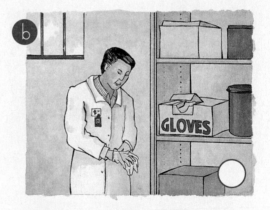

Performance Check

1. Write

Write coworkers **or** supervisor.

a. _____   b. _____   c. _____

2. Write.

Complete the dialog.

| Hi | meet | Nice |

A _____ , I'm Elena.

B Nice to _____ you, Elena. I'm Richard.

A _____ to meet you, too, Richard.

3. Write.

Write Thank you **or** I'm sorry.

A These towels look great. Good work!

A These copies don't look very good. Please copy the forms again.

B _____ , Mrs. Li.

B _____ , Ms. West. I'll copy them again now.

Look at the pictures.

Name the jobs.

What are some other workplaces?

Where do you work?

Getting Started

Match.

2. Work with a partner.

**Which job can you do? Circle the picture.
Show your partner.**

Unit 10   111

Jobs

1. Practice the dialog.

A I want a job.
B What job do you do want?
A I want a job as a cook.

2. Work with a partner.

Say the names of the jobs.

a. painter

b. custodian

c. cook

d. clerk

e. mechanic

f. housekeeper

3. Circle.

Circle PAINTER, CUSTODIAN, HOUSEKEEPER, **and** MECHANIC. **Say the words.**

Department of Employment Services

(PAINTER WANTED)

Riverside
Apartments
555-6010

HELP WANTED
HOUSEKEEPER

Greenway Motel
555-8900

**MECHANIC
WANTED**

Rick's Auto
Body Shop
555-0734

HELP WANTED
CUSTODIAN

Chicago Public
Schools
555-7711

4. Write.

Write the jobs. Say the jobs.

a. _housekeeper_

b. _____

c. _____

5. Complete the sentence.

A What job do you want?

B I want a job as a _____.

6. Work with a partner.

Practice the dialog in 5.

1. Practice the dialog.

A I want to apply for the job.
B Do you have any experience?
A Yes, I do. I was a cook from 1995 to 1998.
B OK, please complete this application.

2. Complete the sentence.

I was a _____ from _____ to _____ .

3. Write the sentence in 2.

I _____ .

I _____ .

4. Listen.

Do they have any experience? Circle yes **or** no.

a. (yes)   no   b.   yes   no

c. yes   no   d.   yes   no

e. yes   no   f.   yes   no

Circle Experience **and** Application. **Say the words.**

Job Application

Name: Wendy Chan			Telephone Number: (712) 555-8734	
Address: 2803 Hilltop Lane, Apt. 21, Sacramento, CA 97521				

Work Experience

From	To	Job	Employer
1995	1998	Clerk	Ming Exports
1990	1994	Housekeeper	County Hospital

6. Write.

Look at the application in 5. Answer the questions.

a. When was Wendy Chan a clerk?

From 1995 to 1998

b. Where was she a clerk?

_____

7. Write.

Complete the application.

Job Application

Name:		Telephone Number:	
Address:			

Work Experience

From	To	Job	Employer

Unit 10

115

1. Practice the dialog.

A Can you work nights?
B Yes, I can.
A Can you work weekends?
B No, I can't. I'm sorry.
A When can you start?
B Immediately.
A OK, be here tonight at 5:00.

2. Complete the sentences.

Write days, nights, **or** weekends.

I can work _____.

I can't work _____.

3. Listen.

Circle the word you hear.

a.   days   (nights)   b.   nights   weekends

c.   days   weekends   d.   days   nights

e.   nights   weekends   f.   days   weekends

4. Circle.

Circle days, nights, **and** weekends.

Name: David Bukowski	Telephone Number: (415) 555-2468
Address: 645 Western Ave. San Francisco, CA 92342	

Availability

Can you work weekends ?	(Yes)	No
Can you work (days) ?	(Yes)	No
Can you work nights ?	(Yes)	No

When can you start work?

Immediately   (In two weeks)   Other date: _____

5. Circle.

Look at the application in 4. Circle the answers.

a. Can David work days?   (yes)   no

b. Can David work weekends?   yes   no

c. Can David work nights?   yes   no

d. When can he start?   immediately   in two weeks

6. Complete the form.

Name:	Telephone Number:
Address:	

Availability

Can you work weekends?	Yes	No
Can you work days?	Yes	No
Can you work nights?	Yes	No

When can you start work?

Immediately   In two weeks   Other date: _____

Unit 10

1. Read.

a
HELP WANTED

Custodian-
Smith Office Supplies
Part time
5:00-9:00/M-F

Experience required.
$6.00 an hour.

Apply in person.
8868 Mountain Road

b
HELP WANTED

Painter wanted.

•

**No experience
necessary.**

•

**Full time,
8:00-4:00**

•

**Call Perfect Painting
555-0012**

2. Write.

Read the sentences. Write the letter of the ad.

a. The ad is for a custodian.   Ad   _a_

b. No experience is necessary for this job.   Ad   ____

c. The job is full time.   Ad   ____

d. The ad is for a painter.   Ad   ____

e. Experience is required for this job.   Ad   ____

f. The job is part time.   Ad   ____

3. Write.

Which job do you want?

Job applied for:

_____

4. Circle.

Circle HELP WANTED, Full time, Part time, Experience, **and** experience. **Say the words.**

HELP WANTED

COOK WANTED.
Experience required.
Full time weekends and nights.
$8.00 an hour.
Tasty Plate Diner, 37 Stuart Street

HELP WANTED

HOUSEKEEPER
No experience necessary.
Part time days.
$5.75 an hour.
Call Mercy Hospital: 555-0301

5. Write.

Apply for a job in 4. Complete the application.

Availability

Job applied for: _____

When can you start work?

Immediately   In two weeks   Other date: _____

Can you work weekends?	Yes	No
Can you work days?	Yes	No
Can you work nights?	Yes	No

Extension

1. Circle.

Look at the ads. Circle the job you want.

Mechanic needed- Joe's Car Repair Full time position. $13.00 an hour. Experience required. 7 Unity Street.	**Painter-** Dale's Painting Service Part time position. Experience preferred. $9.00 an hour. Call 555-2018.

2. Write.

Complete the application.

JOB APPLICATION

Name: _____

Address: _____

_____

_____

Telephone Number: _____

Position Applied For:

WORK EXPERIENCE

From	To	Job	Employer

AVAILABILITY

Can you work days?	❏ Yes ❏ No	When can you start work?
Can you work nights?	❏ Yes ❏ No	❏ Immediately
Can you work weekends?	❏ Yes ❏ No	❏ In two weeks

Performance Check

1. Write.

Complete the application.

MERCY HOSPITAL   APPLICATION FOR EMPLOYMENT

Name: _____   Telephone Number: _____

Address: _____

City: _____   State: _____   Zip Code: _____

Position Applied For: _____

When can you start?   ❑ Immediately   ❑ In two weeks
When can you work?   ❑ Days   ❑ Nights   ❑ Weekends

WORK EXPERIENCE			
From	To	Job	Employer

2. Circle.

Read the sentences. Circle the ad.

ⓐ MECHANIC WANTED

Good Wrench Garage
$12 an hour, full-time.
Experience required.

ⓑ COOK WANTED

Sandy's Hamburgers
Part time, $7.50 an hour.
No experience required.

1. The ad is for a mechanic.   Ad a   Ad b

2. The job is part time.   Ad a   Ad b

3. Experience is required for this job.   Ad a   Ad b

4. The ad is for a cook.   Ad a   Ad b

Unit 10   121

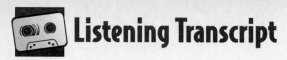 

Listening Transcript

UNIT 1

Page 5

Exercise 4. Listen.

Circle the word you hear.

a. A: What's your last name?
   B: My last name's Reyna. R-E-Y-N-A.

b. A: What's her name?
   B: Her name's Eva.

c. A: Please write your last name on
      the form.
   B: Excuse me?
   A: Please write your last name.

d. A: Tell me your first name again,
      please.
   B: My first name's Leonard.
   A: Nice to meet you, Leonard.

Page 6

Exercise 3. Listen.

Circle the word you hear.

a. A: What's your address?
   B: My address is 42 River Street.

b. A: What number building does Gloria
      work in?
   B: Number 307.

c. A: What street is the warehouse on?
   B: I think it's on Water Street.

d. A: Do you know the address of the
      eye clinic?
   B: Yes, the address is 22 Lakeshore
      Drive. It's next to the hospital.

Page 8

Exercise 3. Listen.

Circle the words you hear.

a. A: What state are we shipping this
      package to?
   B: The state? California.

b. A: Do you know the zip code?
   B: The zip code is 93365.

c. A: What city are you flying from?
   B: Miami.
   A: And what city are you flying to?
   B: New York.

Page 10

Exercise 3. Listen.

Do you hear *telephone number*?
Circle *yes* or *no*.

a. A: What's Arthur's telephone number?
   B: I don't know his telephone number,
      but I can look it up for you.

b. A: What's the address for our next
      delivery?
   B: 18 Main Street.

c. A: Do you have the telephone number
      for Apex Shoe Repair?
   B: Wait a minute. I have it right here.
      It's 555-6767.

d. A: In order to complete this job
      application, we'll need your telephone
      number.
   B: I don't have a telephone right now,
      but I can give you my uncle's
      telephone number if that's all right.
   A: Of course. That'll be fine.

e. A: Is there a telephone number where we
      can reach you in case of emergency?
   B: Yes, the telephone number is
      555-1267.
   A: Thanks.

f. A: The pet clinic is on Town Road.
   B: What number?
   A: Number fourteen.

UNIT 2

Page 16

Exercise 3. Listen.

Circle the place you hear.

a. A: I'm here to paint Mr. Higgins' office. Can you tell me where it is?
   B: Mr. Higgins' office? It's over there on the right.

b. A: We need to move these tables to the break room.
   B: That should be easy to do. The break room isn't far.

c. A: Excuse me. Do you know where the exit is?
   B: Yes, the exit's at the end of the hall, on the left.
   A: On the left? Thanks.

d. A: I can't find the ladies' room on this map.
   B: There's a ladies' room straight ahead on the right and another one on the second floor.
   A: Thanks.

Page 18

Exercise 3. Listen.

Circle the word you hear.

a. A: Where do you want me to hang this poster?
   B: On the right.
   A: On the right near the window?
   B: Yes, that'll be fine.

b. A: Where are the pay phones?
   B: They're down the hall on the left.
   A: On the left. Thanks.

c. A: Is the break room up ahead on the left?
   B: Yes, it's on the left, next to room 25.

d. A: Where's the exit?
   B: It's on the right, just past the soda machines. You can't miss it.

Page 20

Exercise 3. Listen.

Do you hear supply room? Circle yes or no.

a. A: We're out of garbage bags. Are there any in the supply room?

B: Yes, there are. Do you want me to get some for you?

b. A: Could you bring me some sponges from the supply room?
   B: Sure, how many?
   A: Oh, about half a dozen.

c. A: Take these towels to the cafeteria as soon as you can.
   B: Sure, I'll do it right away.

Page 22

Exercise 3. Listen.

Look at the picture in 1. Circle yes or no.

a. A: I need some large bags.
   B: Bags are on the top shelf. I can get them for you.

b. A: I'm looking for some notebooks.
   B: All the notebooks are on the middle shelf. See them over there?
   A: Yes, I do. On the middle shelf.

c. A: Can you help me? I need the towels, but they're on the top shelf and I can't reach that high.
   B: Sure, I can help you. How many towels do you need?

d. A: Are there any envelopes in here?
   B: Yes, there's a box of envelopes on the top shelf.
   A: Are you sure?

e. A: Where are the gloves?
   B: Look on the bottom shelf. I just put some there.
   A: OK, thanks.

f. A: Do you know where the paper is?
   B: Yes, there's paper on the bottom shelf.
   A: On the bottom shelf? You're right.

UNIT 3

Page 28

Exercise 3. Listen.

Circle the word you hear.

a. A: I can't pull this cord.
B: You need to unlock the safety latch. Then you should be able to pull it easily.

b. A: Which button do I push to start the scanner?
B: Push this button to start. Push the button next to it to stop.

c. A: How do I put this in reverse?
B: Turn the key. Then push down on the pedal.

d. A: I can't get this sewing machine to start. Can you help me?
B: Sure. Before you can start this machine, you have to pull the lever.
A: Oh, I see. Thanks.

e. A: Marty wants us to take this cart back to housekeeping.
B: All right, I'll pull it if you get the door.

f. A: Help me push this desk over by the wall.
B: Sure, I'll be right there.

Page 30

Exercise 3. Listen.

Circle the word you hear.

a. A: Is the dishwasher on?
B: Yes, I already turned it on.

b. A: This coffee is cold. Did someone turn off the coffee maker?
B: I don't know, but I can check.

c. A: How do I turn off this dryer?
B: Push STOP. That's the small button on the back.

d. Please read the manual before you start that sander. I don't want any accidents.

e. A: I can't get the microwave oven to start.
B: Did you check to see if it's plugged in?
A: No, I didn't, but I will now.

f. A: Can you turn off the vacuum cleaner for a minute? I think I hear the telephone ringing.

B: Of course I'll turn it off.
A: Thanks.

Page 32

Exercise 3. Listen.

Circle the words you hear.

a. A: How do I replace the bag for this vacuum cleaner?
B: Take out the old bag. Close the top securely.

b. A: Where do I put in the toner?
B: Open the door to the copier. Put the toner in here.

c. A: I can't get this machine to start.
B: Put in the key all the way.
A: I did that.
B: Now turn it to the left.

d. A: The green light on the coffee maker just went on. What should I do?
B: Take out the pot. It's ready to serve.

e. A: How do I get into this computer program?
B: You need to put in your password. Then press ENTER.

f. A: Should I take out the cake?
B: No, don't take it out yet. It should bake a little longer.

Page 34

Exercise 3. Listen.

Circle the word you hear.

a. A: Can I close the trunk now?
B: No, wait a minute. I need to get the tool kit out first. Then you can close it.

b. A: I need you to close the freezer door for me. My hands are full.
B: No problem. I'll close it for you.

c. A: Do you know how to open the door?
B: Yes, just put your ID card on the sensor. The door will open automatically.

d. A: I can't open this gate. Do you know how?

B: Uh-huh. Push this button. See? Now you can open it.

UNIT  4

Page 40

Exercise 3. Listen.

Circle the day you hear.

a. A: Can you work late this Thursday?
    B: No, not this week. I've got a doctor's appointment on Thursday.

b. It feels as if Friday's always our busiest day. I think I make more deliveries on Friday than any other day of the week.

c. A: My son's playing football on Saturday. Can you come to the game?
    B: What time does the game start? I work on Saturday morning.
    A: At 2:00.
    B: Sure, I'll be there.

d. A: Do you know when we get paid next?
    B: On Tuesday.
    A: Tuesday? Thanks.

Page 42

Exercise 3. Listen.

Circle the date you hear.

a. A: When can I see the dentist?
    B: How's November 10?
    A: November 10 isn't good for me. Is there anything available the next week?

b. A: When can you start work?
    B: How's next Monday?
    A: December 13? That'll be fine.
    B: Good, I'll see you on December 13.

c. A: They're installing the new irrigation system on June 25.
    B: June 25 is next Thursday. I didn't realize they were starting work so soon.

d. A: Can you work for me next Wednesday?
    B: July 14?
    A: Yes.
    B: Sure, I'm free on the fourteenth. I'd be happy to help you out.

Page 44

Exercise 3. Listen.

Circle the year you hear.

a. A: Did you start work here in 1997?
    B: Yes, I started on March 30, 1997.

b. A: When did you arrive in the United States?
    B: In 1989.
    A: When exactly?
    B: On July 2, 1989.

c. A: When will you finish your apprentice work?
    B: In September 2001.
    A: Was that 2001?
    B: Yes, and I'm really looking forward to it.

d. A: Just fill in your date of birth and your application form will be complete.
    B: Oh, OK. It's August 10, 1982.

Page 47

Exercise 3. Listen.

Circle the time you hear.

a. A: Excuse me. When does the next train arrive?
    B: It should be here at 4:00.
    A: 4:00? Thanks.

b. A: Wake up! It's 7:30. It's time to get ready for work.
    B: 7:30? Oh, no! I'm late.

c. A: Do you want to meet for lunch today around 12:15?
    B: 12:15's OK. See you then.

d. A: What time should we turn on the lights tonight?
    B: How about 5:45?
    A: 5:45 sounds right to me.

Circle the words you hear.

a. A: Welcome to Nemo's Pizza Shop. May I take your order?

    B: Yes, please. I'd like a large pizza to go.

b. A: Thank you. Here's your change.

    B: I think you still owe me a dollar.

    A: Oh, you're right. Here you are.

    B: Thank you.

c. A: Hello, Northern Construction Company. How may I direct your call?

    B: I'd like to speak to Bill Smith.

    A: One moment, please.

d. A: Thank you for calling Quick Copiers. This is Norman. How can I help you?

    B: I'm calling from Cole Manufacturing. We're having problems with our new copier.

    A: I'll put your call through to our service department.

Page 55

Do you hear *Customer Service*? Circle *yes* or *no*.

a. I bought this ceiling fan here yesterday, and I'm having trouble getting it to work. I'd like to exchange it. Can you tell me where the customer service department is?

b. A: May I help you?

    B: I think so. The starter on this mower isn't working correctly.

    A: Let me call my manager. He can help you with that.

c. A: Is there something I can do for you?

    B: I'd like to return this microwave oven.

    A: Customer Service takes care of all returns. Just walk straight ahead to the back of the store.

    B: Thanks.

d. A: Can I help you?

    B: There's something wrong with this battery. It won't take a charge.

    A: You need to go to Customer Service. Someone there can take care of you.

Page 56

Circle the word you hear.

a. A: Do you know how much these boxes are? There's no price on them.

    B: I'm sorry. Let me check on that for you.

b. A: Excuse me. This coffee has milk and sugar in it. I asked for it black.

    B: I'm sorry, ma'am. I'll get you a fresh cup of black coffee right away.

    A: Thank you.

c. A: I've enjoyed talking to you about job opportunities. Goodbye and thank you.

    B: It was my pleasure, George. Good luck in your job hunt.

d. A: This is Ernest Chang in room 508. There aren't any towels in the bathroom.

    B: I'm sorry, Mr. Chang. I'll send someone up with towels right away.

Page 58

Circle the word you hear.

a. A: Would you like to return these speakers?

    B: Yes, I would. And I'd like a refund, please.

    A: Just complete this form and I can give you your refund.

b. A: This can opener doesn't work. I'd like to exchange it for a new one.

    B: I'd be happy to exchange it for you. Do you have the receipt?

    A: Yes, I've got the receipt right here.

c. A: I've got to return this ladder. Can I get a refund for it?

B: Of course you can. Just fill out and sign this form.

d. A: Good morning.
B: Good morning. I'd like to exchange these gloves for a smaller size.
A: OK, I can exchange those gloves for you. What size do you need?

U N I T 6

Page 64

Exercise 3. Listen.

Circle the words you hear.

a. A: What time do I have to come in tomorrow, Rita?
B: Let me check the appointment book. . . .You've got a cut and color at 8:00.
A: OK, I'll be in early.

b. A: Hello, Family Bakery.
B: Hi, Martha. This is Rasheed. My dentist appointment was canceled, so I'll be in on time today.
A: Good. Thanks for calling, Rasheed.

c. A: Good morning, Uptown Catering.
B: Dorothy? This is Bill Gordon. I'm sorry, but I'm going to be late today. My car won't start. I should be there in about 25 minutes.
A: OK, Bill. See you then.

d. A: This is Carey Miller. I can't come to the phone right now, but please leave me a message and I'll return your call as soon as possible. Thank you.
B: Hi, Carey. This is Antonio. Can you cover for me at the restaurant Monday afternoon? I need to pick up my daughter at day care, and I might be a little late. Give me a call. My number's 555-4336. Thanks.

Page 66

Exercise 3. Listen.

Do you hear *repeat?* Circle *yes* or *no*.

a. A: The telephone number at the training center is 555-9288.
B: Can you repeat that?
A: Sure, it's 555-9288.

b. A: I need 100 copies of this report for the staff meeting this afternoon.
B: OK, I'll get started on them now.
A: Thank you.

c. A: Jack up the car and rotate the tires.
B: I'm sorry. What did you say?
A: Wait a minute. I'll show you.

d. A: You're in charge of cleaning rooms 102 and 108.
B: Which rooms? Could you repeat the numbers?
A: Sure, 102 and 108.

e. A: The meeting is at 12:30 in the board room.
B: OK, I'll tell the others.
A: Thanks.

f. A: Where are we taking this order?
B: 88 East Eighth Street.
A: Excuse me?
B: I'm sorry. That is kind of confusing. Let me repeat that for you. It's 88 East Eighth Street.

Page 70

Exercise 3. Listen.

Circle the word you hear.

a. A: Emilio, how do you get to work so early?
B: I take the express bus.

b. A: How do you come to work?
B: I walk almost every day. I live near here and, of course, it's great exercise.

c. A: Can you drive me to the store tomorrow?
B: I'm sorry. I can't. My car's in the shop getting fixed.

d. If we want to take the bus, we'd better hurry. It leaves in ten minutes.

e. A: I'm calling about the ad for a delivery person.
B: Can you drive a truck?

A: Yes, I can.
B: Good. Would you like to come in later today for an interview?

f. A: It's a beautiful day. Let's walk downtown for a change.
B: OK, walking sounds like fun.

UNIT 7

Page 76

Exercise 3. Listen.

Circle the amount you hear.

a. A: Will that be cash or check?
B: What was the total again?
A: $21.90.
B: $21.90? I think I'll pay cash.

b. A: This paint is on sale for $15.10.
B: $15.10? That's not much of a sale.

c. A: All together that comes to $13.60.
B: $13.60? Will you take a check for that?

d. A: I think you gave me too much change. I should get $7.40 back.
B: You're right. Thank you. Your change should be $7.40.

e. A: The work boots in this catalog are $65.00 a pair.
B: Oh, I didn't know that work boots cost $65.00.

f. A: The electric bill this month was $32.88.
B: $32.88? That's less than it was last month.

Page 79

Exercise 3. Listen.

Write *cash* or *check*.

a. A: How much is a case of cat food?
B: $15.95.
A: $15.95? I guess I'll pay for that in cash.

b. A: Your total comes to $21.50. How would you like to pay?
B: Can I write a check?
A: Yes, but I'll need to see some ID.

c. A: I'm sorry. We only accept cash.
B: OK, I think I have enough cash with me. What was the total again?

d. A: Harold's requires a 20% deposit on all layaways.
B: Will you accept a check for that?
A: A check will be fine.

Page 81

Exercise 3. Listen.

Do they ask for ID? Circle *yes* or *no*.

a. A: I'll need to see some ID, please.
B: Some ID? Here's my driver's license.

b. Please complete this application, sign it, and bring it back to me when you're done.

c. A: Did you sign the check?
B: Yes, I signed the check and wrote my account number on the back.

d. A: May I see your ID?
B: Yes, here's my passport.

Page 83

Exercise 3. Listen.

Do you hear *deposit*? Circle *yes* or *no*.

a. A: I'd like to deposit this check.
B: OK, please fill out this deposit slip.

b. A: Has my deposit of $362.44 cleared yet?
B: Yes, that deposit cleared yesterday.

c. A: Will that be cash, check, or charge?
B: Check. What was the total again?
A: All together it came to $25.32.

d. A: Do you want to deposit this to your checking or savings account?
B: Savings, please.
A: OK, then you need to fill out this deposit slip.

e. A: Did you deposit your paycheck yet?
B: No, not yet. I was going to deposit it on my way home today.

f. A: May I help you?

Listening Transcript

B: I'd like to cash this check.
A: Do you have an account with this bank?
B: Yes, I do.

Page 85

Exercise 3. Listen.

Circle the amount you hear.

a. A: If we change the oil and replace the windshield wipers, it'll cost you $27.98.
B: $27.98? OK, go ahead and do it.

b. A: All the winter coats are now $48.00.
B: Men's and women's coats?
A: Yes, mark them all $48.00.

c. A: How much extra would it cost to send this package overnight?
B: $14.10.
A: $14.10's kind of high. I'll send it regular mail.

d. A: All together the calendars you ordered come to $55.15.
B: You'll take a purchase order for $55.15, won't you?

e. A: Jack needs to be more careful when he's working. It cost $30.25 to replace that broken window.
B: Only $30.25? I thought it'd be more than that.

f. A: Here's your change. $11.11.
B: Are you sure that's correct?
A: Let me check. . . .Yes, ma'am. $11.11's your change.

UNIT 8

Page 88

Exercise 3. Listen.

Circle the word you hear.

a. A: What happened?
B: He slipped on the wet floor.
A: Is he OK?
B: No, he isn't. He hurt his arm. I think we should take him to the emergency room.

b. A: What's the matter with your hand?
B: I cut it on this glass. It hurts a little.
A: It's not a bad cut. I'll wash it and put on a bandage.

c. A: The doctor says my arm is broken.
B: What happened?
A: I was carrying a lot of heavy boxes, and I wasn't watching where I was going.

d. A: What's the problem?
B: My back hurts.
A: How long has it hurt?
B: For a few days now.

Page 90

Exercise 3. Listen.

Circle the words you hear.

a. A: You can't smoke in here.
B: Why not?
A: The sign says NO SMOKING.

b. A: Be careful with that box. It contains poison.
B: You know, this box really should be labeled more carefully.

c. A: Watch out! Didn't you see the DANGER sign?
B: No, I didn't. Thanks for the warning.

d. A: Did you see the NO SMOKING sign?
B: No, I didn't, but I'm glad they put one up. Someone could start a fire here very easily.

e. A: That barrel contains poison, so be careful when you move it.
B: Good point. I'd better put on my safety gear.

f. Make sure no one goes in that door marked DANGER. They're doing some testing in there right now.

Page 92

Exercise 3. Listen

Circle the word you hear.

a. A: There's a fire in the kitchen!
B: A fire? Call 911!

b.
A: I'd like to report an accident.
B: What's the location?
A: The accident's in front of 19 Sergeant Street.
B: We'll send help right away.

c.
A: Is that the fire alarm?
B: Yes, it is. And I smell smoke.
A: Let's get out of the building now!

d.
A: There's been an accident.
B: What happened?
A: Gino fell down the stairs. There's an ambulance on its way.

e.
A: Where's the accident?
B: On Broad Street. A car ran a red light.
A: Broad Street? We can be there in five minutes.

f.
A: Has anyone shown you where the fire exits are?
B: No, not yet.

Page 95

Exercise 3. Listen.

What do the people do? Circle.

a.
A: John burned his hand.
B: I think he needs to go to the hospital. City Hospital isn't far and I can drive.

b.
A: She's unconscious. Call 911 right away.
B: I already called 911. They're sending an ambulance.

c.
A: Lisa fell and hit her head. What should we do?
B: Don't move her. I'll call 911.

d.
A: Christy just fainted. Do you think she needs to go to the hospital?
B: Yes, I do. I think a doctor should look at her.

UNIT 9

Page 101

Exercise 3. Listen.

Circle the word you hear.

a.
A: Excuse me. I'm looking for the supervisor.
B: That would be Susan. She's over there by the door.
A: Thanks.

b.
A: Have you met your coworkers yet?
B: My coworkers? No, I haven't met them.
A: OK, let me take you around and introduce you to them.

c.
A: I'm not sure what I should do now.
B: I think your coworkers are loading the trucks over there.
A: Thanks.

d.
A: Did you find out what to do?
B: No, we haven't.
A: Your supervisor should have the work orders.
B: I'll go find him. Do you know where he is?

Page 103

Exercise 3. Listen.

**Do you hear *Nice to meet you?*
Circle *yes* or *no*.**

a.
A: Pedro, this is Sandra.
B: Nice to meet you, Sandra.
C: Nice to meet you, Pedro.

b.
Hi, Ming. I'm Julia. It's nice to meet you. I've heard a lot of good things about you from your boss at the warehouse.

c.
A: I don't think we've met. I'm Steve.
B: Nice to meet you, Steve. I'm Katya. I'm so glad to be working here at the shelter. What can I do to get started?

d.
A: Where are you from, Carmen?
B: I'm from Houston.
A: Oh, really? I'm from Houston, too.

Page 105

Exercise 3. Listen.

Circle the words you hear.

a.
A: Karen, when's our afternoon break?
B: 2:30.

A: 2:30? Good. That's only a few minutes from now.

b. A: All of the employees in this division get a morning break at 9:30.
B: So everyone takes their morning break at the same time?
A: That's right.

c. A: Do we get a break in the afternoon?
B: Yes, there's an afternoon break at 3:00.
A: OK, do you want to meet then?

d. Can I take an early lunch today? I'd like to go to my daughter's school and have lunch with her.

Page 107

Page 107

Exercise 3. Listen.

Do you hear *Good work?* **Circle** *yes* **or** *no.*

a. A: Did you work on these dresses?
B: Yes, I did.
A: They look beautiful. Good work.
B: Thank you, Ms. Phillips.

b. A: Please wash these glasses again, Jill. They have spots on them.
B: I'm sorry. I'll wash them now.

c. A: Good work on painting this room, Ken.
B: Thanks, I'll tell Eddie you said so. He was a real help to me on this job.

d. A: You finished these reports early? Good work, Mary.
B: Thank you, Ms. Kelly.

UNIT 10

Page 114

Exercise 4. Listen.

Do they have any experience?

a. A: I'm calling about the ad for a gardener.
B: Do you have any experience?
A: Yes, before I came to this country, I was a gardener for many years.
B: Good. Can you come in later today

for an interview?
A: Sure.

b. A: General Hospital. May I help you?
B: Yes, I saw your ad for a housekeeper. I'd like to apply for the job. Can you tell me about it?
A: Well, it's a part time position, and the salary's $6.25 an hour. Do you have any experience?
B: No, I don't. Is that a problem?
A: No, it's OK. Experience isn't required. We have a training program for people without experience.
B: That sounds great.

c. A: Look at this ad, May. It's a perfect job for you.
B: What kind of job is it?
A: The American Cafe's looking for a full time cook with experience working in a restaurant.
B: That sounds perfect. I have three years of experience working at the Pickwick Restaurant. Is there a phone number I can call?
A: Here.

d. A: I'm interested in applying for the clerk's job.
B: Tell me, do you have any experience?
A: No, I don't have experience as a clerk, but I'm very organized and I enjoy office work.
B: All right, please fill out this form.
A: Thank you.

e. A: Hello, I'm here about your ad for a painter.
B: Do you have experience as a painter?
A: No, I don't have any experience, but I want to learn.
B: Well, that's OK. We prefer experience but don't require it.

f. A: I need to find a job.
B: Here's a Help Wanted ad for a custodian.
A: Really? I have experience as a custodian. Who's the job with?
B: The city school system. They want people with experience, so it sounds like a good job for you.

Page 116

Circle the word you hear.

a. A: We need a cook who can work
      nights.
   B: I can work nights.
   A: That's good. Could you start Friday
      night?
   B: Yes, Friday night's fine.

b. A: Why do you want to work weekends?
   B: I go to school, so weekends are the
      best time for me to work.
   A: Oh, you're a student. We hire a lot
      of students.

c. A: Look, John, this ad is for a mechanic
      who can work days from nine to
      five.
   B: Days from nine to five? That's just
      what I'm looking for.
   A: Here's the ad.
   B: Thanks, I'll call them right away.

d. A: Do you have any positions open
      that are days only?
   B: Yes, we do. This is the list of
      positions that are days only.
   A: May I have a look at that?
   B: Certainly. Here you are.

e. A: Can you work nights?
   B: Yes, that's fine.
   A: Oh, good. We have a hard time
      finding people who can work
      nights.

f. A: The only time I can't work is on
      weekends.
   B: Actually, we're not open on
      weekends, so that's not a problem.
      Can you start this week?
   A: Sure thing.

Vocabulary

UNIT 1

name
first name
last name

address
number
street

city
state
zip code

telephone number

UNIT 2

break room
exit
ladies' room
men's room
office
supply room

left
right

top
middle
bottom

bags
envelopes
gloves
notebooks
paper
towels

UNIT 3

coffee maker
copier
dishwasher
dryer
microwave oven
vacuum cleaner
washing machine

pull
push

on
off
start
stop

put in
take out

close
open

UNIT 4

Sunday
Monday
Tuesday
Wednesday
Thursday
Friday
Saturday
Sunday

date
today
tomorrow

date of birth
month
year

January
February
March
April
May
June
July
August
September
October
November
December

time

UNIT 5

please
thank you

customer service
hello

goodbye
sorry

exchange
refund

UNIT 6

early
late
on time

repeat
understand

careful
quiet
Work Zone

drive
take
walk

UNIT 7

penny
dime
nickel
quarter

$
dollar
cents
change

cash
check

ID
paycheck
sign

deposit

UNIT 8

arm
back
eye
foot
hand
leg

broken
cut
hurt

danger
no smoking
poison

911
accident
fire

emergency room
hospital

UNIT 9

coworkers
supervisor

Nice to meet you.
Where are you from?

break
lunch

good work

UNIT 10

clerk
cook
custodian
housekeeper
mechanic
painter

application
experience

days
nights
weekends

full time
help wanted
part time